CONTENT

Editor: Michael Whitehouse
Deputy Editor: Russell Whitehouse
Publisher: Paul Appleton
Design: Debbie Walker,
Steve Diggle, Matt Chapman,
Dominique Maynard
Advertising: David Smith
Managing Director: Adrian Cox
Commercial Director: Ann Saundry
Marketing: Kirsty Flatt

www.keypublishing.com

Printing: Warners (Midlands) plc,
The Maltings, Bourne, Lincs. PE10 9PH

ISBN: 978 0 946219 40 7

© Key Publishing Ltd, May 2013

Registered Office: Key Publishing Ltd,
Units 1-4 Gwash Way Industrial Estate,
Ryhall Road, Stamford, PE9 1XP.

Cover: **No. 4 *Palmerston* shunts
slate wagons at Porthmadog
Harbour Station.**

This page: **No.8 *Fenella* and No.4 *Loch*
climb the bank at Keristal on the
Isle of Man Railway in April 2011.**

Celebrating the
BRITISH NARROW GAUGE RAILWAY

In the 1950s we lived at 344 Lordswood Road, Harborne, Birmingham 17, an address which all the members of the Talyllyn Railway Society knew as my father was the first society secretary. So, our house was always full of railways and railway people; it was just part of life. Lord Northesk, President of the Talyllyn, Adolf Giesel, inventor of the Giesel ejector chimney, James Boyd, the historian and Ian Allan, the publisher were all frequent visitors for dinner. The bookcases were full of railway books, including the early Boyd and Kidner volumes and PBW had started to write his own books with *Narrow Gauge Album* being one of the first on the bookshelf.

Our early holidays were inextricably bound round the resurgence of the Talyllyn Railway in Mid Wales. We stayed first with Mrs Jones at Dolgoch Falls and then upgraded to the Trefeddian Hotel just outside Aberdovey. I rode behind *Edward Thomas* and *Douglas* on the TR, watched the Sundays-only train to Barmouth behind a 45XX tank and, whilst PBW was having seemingly interminable conversations with grown ups, I explored Wharf and Pendre stations. I spent many happy hours 'driving' the original *Talyllyn* forlorn in the Pendre barn, as well as museum exhibits *George Henry* and *Russell*; together we covered many miles up the Fathew Valley, around the quarries and along the Welsh Highland in my mind. For you see, even at a very young age, I knew all these railways. They were often in the forefront of my life: in conversation with people, on 16mm film or featured in the many

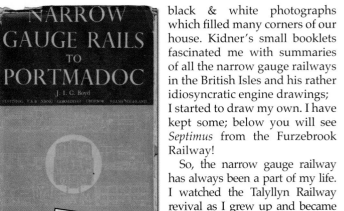

black & white photographs which filled many corners of our house. Kidner's small booklets fascinated me with summaries of all the narrow gauge railways in the British Isles and his rather idiosyncratic engine drawings; I started to draw my own. I have kept some; below you will see *Septimus* from the Furzebrook Railway!

So, the narrow gauge railway has always been a part of my life. I watched the Talyllyn Railway revival as I grew up and became a teenager: *Talyllyn* left the Pendre barn for repair and came back to work. In the late 1950s, we ventured further north to Portmadoc for a very wet Whitsun and I had my first ride, but only to Penrhyn, behind *Taliesin*; I remember being intrigued by this extraordinary articulated engine having two chimneys and two regulators and longing to ride behind it further up the line which I knew still existed. When the FR was rebuilt to Tany-y-Bwlch I 'made' PBW walk with me all the way to Dduallt and back, fascinated by the prospect of the line coming back to life and I thoroughly enjoyed every minute of University vacations at Boston Lodge and learning to fire ex-Penryhn Railway *Blanche*.

I quickly learned about the spread of narrow gauge railways overseas from my first visit to the Reseau Breton Railway in Brittany, the Swiss mountain rack railways (which looked very similar to the Snowdon Mountain Railway, or was it the other

Septimus

Above: **Prince at Harbour Station in August 2005, the 50th anniversary of the FR's revival, with a recreation of the original 1955 train to Boston Lodge halt.**

Narrow Gauge Inspirations: *Narrow Gauge Rails to Portmadoc* **book front cover, front cover of Kidner's** *English Narrow Gauge Railways* **and the cover of** *Narrow Gauge Railways of North Wales,* **another Kidner classic.**

way round?). Then, in the early 1970s, we ventured further afield and I was thrilled to see the Beyer Garratts of Africa, both the 4-6-4+4-6-4 15th Class on the international mail train from Bulawayo to Mafeking and the smaller NGG16 2-6-2+2-6-2 Garratts on the South African Natal sugar lines. Soon, it wasn't long before I saw the hill railways in India with the two foot Scottish-built North British tank engines climbing noisily up and around impossible curves up towards the sky and, also, the last Beyer Peacock steam tram fussing along the Indonesian highway in Surabaya shrieking on its high pitch whistle as it swung across the road.

In the space of a few years, I had heard and seen at first hand the spectrum of British narrow gauge railways, what they did and how they changed the world by opening up the hinterland to the sea and facilitating trade and the economy of foreign lands to flourish. This story starts at home for me and, by home, I mean just that - not just my country. So, we will use that framework to celebrate the British narrow gauge story. 2013 is a good time to do so for the catalyst is the 150th anniversary of steam locomotives on the Ffestiniog Railway in the 'top left hand corner of Wales'. The FR was not the first narrow gauge railway, nor the first to introduce steam engines; but it was the first to introduce steam traction as its principal motive power on so small a gauge and widely promote it to the world

with panache. As such, the railway has caught the imagination of many as it continues its tradition of innovation, spreads similar techniques and ideas to the world at large and, cleverly, brings the subject full circle by re-importing several of the last type of narrow gauge engine Britain ever made for export to run on its associated and reconstructed Welsh Highland Railway. This year in North Wales you will be able to see the very first FR steam engine alongside the very last Beyer Garratt ever made in England for export. Don't miss it!

Michael Whitehouse

Below: ***Princess*, the Ffestiniog Railway's first steam engine and 150 years old in 2013, stands outside Boston Lodge Works against a Snowdonia backdrop having been cosmetically restored for her sesquicentenary.**
Photo: Glenn Williams

RACEHORSES
from Wales

Racehorses are usually the preserve of the very rich or, at least, consortia of folk who have money to spare. They require detailed attention, training and exercise. When racing they draw the attention of the world, especially in the famous Grand National.

The Assheton Smith family owned and raced several racehorses as a hobby. They also owned the Dinorwic quarry in North Wales, one of the largest in the world and, together with the nearby quarries at Bethesda and Blaeunau Ffestiniog, the North Wales region produced some of the best roofing slates in the world and were exported everywhere. The roof of Westminster Hall is fitted out with their best. It was a good trade and it made money.

King of the Scarlets seen here repainted by the Dinorwic Quarry workshop before export to the USA. This engine has recently been repatriated by Graham Lee and can be seen at Statfold Barn

George B blowing off steam in the Dinorwic Quarry. This engine was purchased privately for preservation and first moved to Ashchurch where it was initially displayed; it is now under restoration and we await seeing him steam once again.

No.1 with a domed boiler blowing off steam in the Dinorwic Quarry.

The essence of Dinorwic: *Holy War* buffering up to a train of slate waste.

Velinheli seen against the backdrop of a huge slate wall in working Dinorwic Quarry days but now restored with an unauthentic copper cap chimney and normally running on the Launceston Steam Railway in Cornwall, which is entirely operated by former Quarry Hunslets.

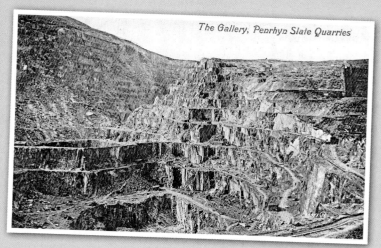

The Gallery, Penrhyn Slate Quarries

Lillian on a slate waggon train at Porthmadog in May 1993.

Sgt Murphy, a Kerr Stuart 0-6-0T (now rebuilt as an 0-6-2T) was retired at Penrhyn quarry in 1955.

Dolbadarn makes her first visit off the Dinorwic system to star on the shuttle service between Porthmadog and Minffordd at the Ffestiniog Railway's 'Hunslet Hundred' gala weekend. Here she is shown leaving Boston Lodge works in her new completely unauthentic yellow ochre livery.

Extracting the slate was a difficult and dangerous operation, involving blasting, tunnelling and opening out chambers within mountains. Local labour was used in thousands to undertake this work in all weathers, requiring long hours and indifferent pay. Many workers died early from silicosis: inhaling deadly slate dust.

To help extract the valuable slate and transport it to the sea, great use was made of narrow gauge railways which have been the subject of much study and erudite research. However, essentially, these railways were laid to the nominal 'two foot' gauge and used a plethora of little steam engines manufactured by the Hunslet Engine Company in Leeds, amongst others. These engines have attracted probably undue attention from enthusiasts. Whilst the workings of the slate quarries and their railways is of interest to industrial archaeologists in its own right, the prospect of personally owning a steam engine lies deep in many enthusiasts hearts and, with the closure of the quarries, many were able to realise their dreams and buy an engine of their own.

All the quarry engines had names. Some were called after family members: *Linda, Blanche, Charles* and *Michael,* but many were named after the Assheton Smith's Grand National winners and other racehorses and provided an eclectic list to read: *Lady Madcap, George B, Maid Marian, Covertcoat, King of the Scarlets* and so caught many peoples' imagination.

The quarry owners were immensely rich, enforced lock outs when strikes for better pay were started and were not unduly concerned about their staff working in poor conditions. So perhaps they really rubbed the noses of their staff in the startling differences between the respective life styles of owners and workers by naming the engines hauling the slate either after themselves or their whims of fancy on the race course. However, the steam engine drivers were proud of the work and looked after their steeds to the best of their ability, often polishing them until they shone and the engines were regarded with great affection.

So, when the Dinorwic quarry finally closed a two day auction was held on 12th & 13th December, 1970 to dispose of all the redundant equipment, enthusiasts flocked to see what they could buy. Whilst many of the preserved railways sought machinery and tools and some came away well satisfied, several individuals with as much cash as they could afford (and possibly more than they could really spare) were able to bid to achieve a lifetime's dream: a steam engine of their very own. For a 'two foot' quarry Hunslet was small enough for one man or a small group to look after and many of the purchases at the auction enabled new lines to be started for pleasure or private use. The second day saw the sale of railway stock and fetched a total of £6,250. Three 1ft 10¾in gauge Hunslets in more-or-less working order fell under the hammer: *Red Damsel* of 1899 fetched £1,550, *Dolbadarn* of 1922 £1,050 and *Wild Aster* of 1904 £700.

This feature is about these survivors and shows their quarry life and also their subsequent life in pictorial

form. That so many of these diminutive narrow gauge engines have survived is not perhaps surprising in the circumstances described. The quarry lasted just long enough in operation for their redundant steam engines and equipment to enter the railway preservation world,

Gwynedd with **Alan Bloom** driving and **PBW** foot-plating on the Bressingham garden circuit.

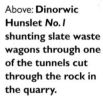

Above: **Dinorwic Hunslet *No.1* shunting slate waste wagons through one of the tunnels cut through the rock in the quarry.**

Left: **Commercial postcard of Penrhyn Quarry entitled 'Men going back to work after dinner, Bethesda',** depicting *Hugh Napier* **on a slate waste train. This engine is now owned by the National Trust and has been restored as a joint venture between Trust and the Ffestiniog Railway, who have finished off the restoration work begun by Penrhyn driver Iorwerth Jones.**

Britomart in steam at the FR's May 1993 'Hunslet Hundred' gala.

Without doubt their story will continue to develop over the years ahead and provide historians with much material for a future history, as much about the people who have restored the engines as about the engines themselves.

The enthusiast world has been fortunate to see many of these engines now at work on private railways and, indeed, become the mainstay of motive power at some of them: the Llanberis Lake Railway (on the trackbed of the four foot Padarn Railway), Bala Lake and Launceston Steam Railways are just three examples. Additionally, the Ffestiniog Railway has become a focal point for collections to be seen in steam and at galas. Perhaps the 'Hunslet Hundred' gala in May 1993 took the biscuit. This was arranged to celebrate the centenary of the Penrhyn Quarry 'main line' two foot Hunslets purchased by the railway in the early 1960s: *Linda* and *Blanche*. This event even brought the third engine of the class *Charles* from Penrhyn Quarry and gathered together many of the smaller port and quarry engines as the pictures show.

which has undoubtedly been richer as a consequence. Even today, the story of the restoration and operation of these little engines is not yet fully told, as recently several have been unearthed from store in the Americas to where they were exported after being bought at auction, once thought to be lost for ever but now brought back to the UK to steam once again.

The Family Reunion

Charles woke from his afternoon nap with a start. He was moving. It was a most peculiar feeling as he hadn't moved for years and years. Soon he was out in the fresh air and being winched onto the back of a lorry. He heard men say that he was going to meet his wife *Blanche* and his daughter *Linda* at a birthday party. *Charles* was all in favour of parties but he had mixed feelings about this one. He was over the moon about the prospect of being on rails again, but rather nervous of meeting the two ladies after all this time. During his long rest at Penrhyn he had heard all sorts of stories on the grapevine about the two ladies in his life, including all manner of fairy tales about them gallivanting around at high speed in all kinds of gaudy colours having had various facelifts. *Charles* was firmly of the opinion that engines should grow old gracefully.

Charles' worksplate.

It was almost like the old days, although the track was a little wide. There were all sorts of quarry engines - some in funny colours - but still it was a party, rather a fancy dress one at that. These modern fashions wouldn't do at all, thought *Charles*; what was wrong with good old fashioned black? It was almost unbelievable to be back with his wife and daughter once again. Unbelievable in two senses. First, the very fact that they were together again. Second, the amazing changes to the ladies' appearance. *Linda* didn't look too bad in her coat of dark blue paint, but what had she been doing to her chimney? And what airs had she taken with her exhaust beat? At least she had retained the shapely lines of her cylinders that *Charles* liked so much. *Blanche*, however,

Charles on display at Boston Lodge.

had completely overdone it and *Charles* told her as much. An outrageous coat of green paint, a thought provoking tender with a cab on it, a go-faster pony truck (*Charles* was prepared to overlook the same fitting on his daughter) and fancy looking cylinders. In fact the only redeeming feature at all was her chimney, and even that was too tall. *Charles* did not approve at all. He cringed when he saw the two of them galloping over the Cob together, double heading a train up into the hills, pandering to the whims of all and sundry. Steam engines were built to do a serious job of work, he thought to himself, and not to go around parading like a couple of ladies of the night.

Still, it was a long time since *Charles* had been in circulation, so to speak, and he had to recognise that engines moved on as it were. Indeed, Centenarians must be pretty fit to run at all. *Charles* liked being the centre of attention at Boston Lodge. He liked being photographed and admired. Talking of being admired, he caught sight of an engine he had not seen for many a year: *Lilla*, a medium sized Quarry Hunslet, whom he remembered from the old days. A nice little engine he thought. The sun came out and *Lilla* puffed around the yard, spending most of her time at Boston Lodge after the party. Perhaps it was a good thing after all that the ladies were out on the line for most of the party...

As if buying and restoring these lovely little engines was not enough, one preservationist, Graham Lee, purchased the trading name of Hunslet and set about making some new examples for sale commercially. Tyseley Locomotive Works were commissioned to build four new boilers, but only two locomotives were actually assembled and neither sold on the open market. Perhaps this was because individuals wanted an original and so they set about with renewed effort to seek out and release those which had been incarcerated in store in the U.S.A. Now virtually every one of the quarry engines has been repatriated and is expected to return to steam.

One final thought remains. Amongst all the preserved remaining 'Quarry Hunslets' there will not be one single 'reference example' left in original untouched condition. This is often a difficult discussion point. Ideally, in museum parlance and taking the word 'preserved' at its dictionary meaning, one example of the type would have been set aside and kept for posterity in original condition, subject perhaps to repainting. This has not happened with the 'Quarry Hunslets' for, although *Rough Pup*, preserved in the Narrow Gauge Railway Museum at Tywyn, has indeed been kept in ex-quarry condition it has now been repainted and so is not quite a 'perfect example'. Whilst it may be unfair to single out some locomotives, the recent repatriation of Dinorwic's *Michael* and *King of the Scarlets* and Penrhyn's *Winifred* from the U.S.A. provided probably a final opportunity to secure an unrestored example. However, their respective owners have (quite understandably) determined that their purchases will return to steam again and so, after a while, they will become - like all the others - just another preserved steam engine from the quarries. *Winifred* from Penrhyn still remains completely as withdrawn from service, including original lined livery and the ash still in the smokebox. A real time warp. But not for long. Although owner, Julian Birley, has decided to undertake a painstakingly careful restoration to working order (including making any new parts to look exactly like those they will replace using the new laser metal printing), his engine will sadly no longer be completely original. That is his prerogative and he is to be applauded for the undoubted hard work undertaken to repatriate the engine at his own cost. Nevertheless, the last chance to keep a Penrhyn engine in totally original condition will have been lost. What will the future say about that?

Top: *Lilla* shunting slate waggons in Minffordd yard.

Above: *Velinheli* and *Alan George* at Boston Lodge.

Left: *Irish Mail*, in action at Boston Lodge in May 1993.

Early memories...

"We stayed with Alan Bloom of Bressingham for a weekend and enjoyed his estate railway running for the public with two Penrhyn Quarry railway engines. PBW and I were privileged to be given a footplate ride on *Gwynedd* with Alan driving on the circuit. Then, when we got back to the station Alan simply got off the footplate and said "enjoy yourselves; you know what to do." PBW and I spent the rest of the afternoon happily taking it in turns to drive and fire *Gwynedd* on the public rides! Fortunately, they are very simple engines and we very quickly learned how to master her!" MW

FOUR FEET GAUGE LOCOMOTIVE "FIRE QUEEN" AT DINORWIC SLATE QUARRIES

Fire Queen

Above: *Fire Queen* emerges into the daylight at Dinorwic Quarry for the first time in 83 years (commercial postcard).

The Dinorwic Quarry railway system was 'two foot', with the track gauge measured as the distance between the centre of one rail to the centre of the other. When the Dinorwic quarry 'main line' between the quarry and port yards was reconstructed to carry more traffic, the gauge was simply doubled to four foot. Although this was an unusual gauge for the British Isles, it had local logic as the narrower gauge slate wagons from the quarries could then simply be carried two abreast on transporter wagons on the larger gauge; slate was a brittle commodity and this helped reduce transhipment damage.

Two engines were purchased in 1848 from A. Horlock of North Fleet Iron Works, a near neighbour of Geo. England in London at a price of £1,500 each. An odd choice of contractor perhaps as Horlock did not specialise in building railway locomotives. Nevertheless, he delivered two steam engines named *Jenny Lind* and *Fire Queen* both built in accordance with T. R. Crampton's patent No. 11,760 of 1847 as

four coupled tender engines. Unusually, the engines had no frames; all wheels and fittings had to be attached to the boiler by individual brackets. The engine had a very long wheelbase and was fitted with Stephenson's valve gear driven by eccentrics on the leading axle.

Jenny Lind was dismantled in 1882 and *Fire Queen* was taken out of service for overhaul in 1886. After the mechanical aspects of the work had been tackled, attention turned to the boiler, which was found to be in worse condition than expected. By that time, two new replacement Hunslet side tanks had arrived and so, reluctantly, management decided to retire *Fire Queen*. Interestingly, work on her simply stopped overnight. The staff had inserted a new boiler tube with only one end expanded before they knocked off shift. The next morning, they were told to stop work and so the other end of the tube has never been expanded to this day! But the engine was not scrapped as she had won affection with the quarry and its owners; rumour has it that the owner's daughter played a leading part in ensuring *Fire Queen* was preserved.

Fire Queen was moved out of the workshops into one of the early 2ft gauge sheds which had large pits and the gauge of the rails was altered to accommodate her. Amazingly, she remained there for 83 years quite safe and sound being regularly cleaned and greased. Then in December 1969 she was brought out of the shed into the sunlight onto temporary track and removed to Penrhyn Castle where she has been repainted for display. A remarkable survivor from a past age.

Top: *Fire Queen* beautifully repainted inside Penrhyn Castle Museum.

Above: *Fire Queen* cylinders and name plate.

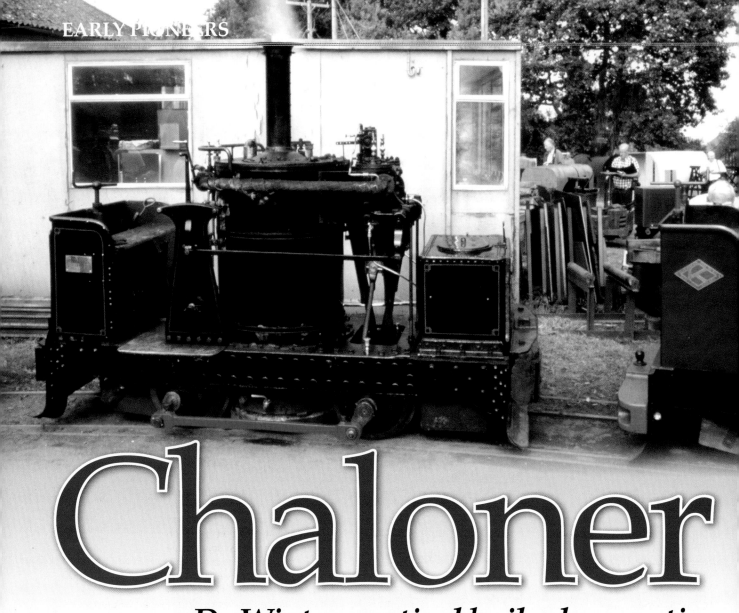

Chaloner

a De Winton vertical boiler locomotive

Above: *Chaloner* in steam at the annual Keef open day on 4th September, 2002.

A letter landed on Alfred Fisher's doorstep on 9th June, 1960 dated the day before. It read: "My directors have decided to let it go for the £21 offered, this means that you will be responsible for all expense in removing the loco from the quarry. Will you please reply by return, and oblige. Yours faithfully, O.G. Williams, General Manager, Pen-yr-Orsedd Slate Quarry Co. Ltd". Alfred had just bought *Chaloner*.

Chaloner was - and still very much is - a De Winton vertical boilered steam engine built by their Union Works in Caernarvon, probably in 1877, but surviving records are not sufficient to be definitive. The engine is a typical example of its type and the only original one remaining in working order, albeit with a new boiler now.

Jeffreys De Winton was an engineer with very varied talents. Most people interested in railway will associate him with this intriguing and highly original vertical boilered narrow gauge steam engine which he designed for the North Wales slate quarries. In fact his design and production output was far more

prodigious that just steam railway engines. It covered the whole range of engineering products needed and used by the various seafaring and quarry industries in North Wales: ships, gas plants, slate cutting machinery, water balances, bridges, girders, steam engines and railway coaches and wagons and anything else which may have been required.

De Wintons were prolific builder of equipment and steam engines for quarries, but by no means the only manufacturers of vertical boilered engines. However, they may perhaps have been the first. Production started in 1868 and was not at all confined to supplies within North Wales and their products were sent to many other parts of Britain as well. Rumour has it that quotes were sent to as far away as India and Easter Island, although no-one has yet come back from there having seen one of his engines and no pictures have yet surfaced - but we live in hope!

Steam engines were made for some thirty years from 1868 to 1897. *Chaloner* was pretty much the end result of a development programme driven by the enormous quarry expansion of the time. After then trade dropped off for two reasons. The quarries had by then been equipped with their basic needs; those which continued to modernise wanted bigger and more powerful engines which De Winton was not geared up to provide, so their ongoing output was subsequently for the smaller quarries.

> *... My directors have decided to let it go for the £21 offered ...*

Chaloner was delivered to Pen-y-Bryn Slate Quarry in the Nantlle Valley. The name derives from one of the quarry directors who lived outside Wales. In 1888, the quarry sold her for £150, half the original purchase price, to Pen-yr-Orsedd Quarry, still in the same valley, where she continued to work for the next 65 years, being occasionally used right up to 1955. It is clear from the quarry's records that she had been maintained during her long period of use and it was this which enabled Alfred Fisher to continue to use the engine in preservation, perhaps the most intriguing part of *Chaloner* life, so enabling subsequent generations to see a De Winton vertical boilered steam engine in use!

Chaloner was taken to Alf's home where there was no initial thinking about running her, that is until several friends, including Teddy Boston, visited Alf and suggested, in no uncertain terms, that there was no point in having a locomotive which did not work. So, after much work and learning about the intricacies of steam engines, the regulator was opened again on 22nd June, 1968 and *Chaloner* was back in business.

Chaloner went to run on the Leighton Buzzard narrow gauge railway, formerly used for sand traffic, but at the time an embryo tourist railway. At a time when British Rail was finishing with its steam engines for ever, Alf Fisher was venturing forth to run *Chaloner* in public passenger service for the first time in the engine's life with the opening day being Saturday 29th June, 1968! A remarkable piece of motive power with which to open a new narrow gauge railway for public consumption! Some initial difficulties, not least with the gauge of the locomotive and the railway, had to be resolved. Not for nothing has the Welsh quarry railway system been called 'nominal two foot'! On examination, *Chaloner* was found to have wheel sets to two different gauges: one foot ten and three quarters and one foot eleven and five eights. The gauge of the sand railway was 'two foot'!

Alf learned how to drive his engine the hard way: "Driving the locomotive proved to be an acquired art and an extraordinarily uncomfortable experience. The engine vibrated severely and the reasons for the hideous chimney extensions seen in quarry days became very obvious. The top of the chimney was exactly at the eye-level of the average height driver and was, moreover, situated less than three feet in front of him. In forward running, smoke and ash drifted back into the faces of the crew, particularly when coasting, and if drivers ended the day with only red eyes and black faces, they were lucky."

Of course, continual use wore the engine out and so a complete strip down and significant repairs became inevitable. The Leighton Buzzard Railway gained additional motive power and so *Chaloner* could be relieved from front line service which she was certainly not suited to. As she reached her centenary, she ventured to other lines and then spent some time on display in the National Railway Museum in York, visited the Ffestiniog Railway and even made a trip to France. Much repair work was undertaken on the FR to great effect, including the fitting of a new all welded boiler. Since then, *Chaloner* has rightly travelled widely so that her owner and supporting team and many people around the country can enjoy this interesting and very different narrow gauge steam engine. She has even been to the Isle of Man to run on the Groudle Glen Railway and has now travelled the whole length of the Ffestiniog and Welsh Highland Railway to boot. It was a proud moment for the team to pose *Chaloner* outside the De Winton erecting shop in Caernarfon on 20th September, 2008.

> ... **National and international exposure of Chaloner has brought the name of De Winton to an audience which would have been inconceivable to her creators ...**
>
> Alfred Fisher, proud owner

Chaloner in steam at Pen-yr-Orsedd Quarry on 26th July, 1950.

Below: **Close up details of *Chaloner* including nameplate, worksplate, chimney and fittings.**

Englands in Wales

the story of the first narrow gauge passenger engines in the British Isles

Above: *The Princess* at Portmadoc Harbour station. The wooden building was subsequently moved to Penrhyn. England did not provide tenders; they were built at Boston Lodge initially using slate wagon parts and probably painted grey.

"The Festiniog Railway Company propose opening their line for traffic by steam on Friday 23rd instant, and intend starting a train from Port Madoc at 10 in the morning..."

It was a brilliantly sunny morning in 1863 and the *North Wales Chronicle* reported the happy day. Two trains were run following each other driven by Charles Holland and George England, the railway's consultant engineer and builder respectively of Britain's first narrow gauge steam engines in passenger service for the public. After the trips, the guests went to the Portmadoc town hall for a gala celebration dinner. The band played, toasts were drunk and speeches were made.

As George England summarised in his dinner speech: "the problem resolved itself into a question of power, high steam pressure at 120 lb/sq inch." The FR's introduction of steam engines was intended to help sustain its profitable monopoly of transporting slate from the Welsh Blaenau Ffestiniog quarries down to the sea, against the proposed introduction of competing railways at a wider gauge than the FR's nominal two foot. Recent history had then already shown that when a new steam operated railway entered the field previously monopolised by a horse drawn railway (as the FR originally was), the latter failed to survive. So, the introduction of steam

locomotives on the FR was most likely done partly out of self defence but also with an eye to increasing traffic.

It was, however, a tremendous achievement! The Festiniog Railway was a world pioneer introducing steam engines on so narrow a gauge. In doing so, it transformed the railway from being a horse drawn tramway into a state of the art railway, leading technology and its development. The concept was to be expanded worldwide. The narrow gauge railways of Europe, the Americas, Africa and Asia all have their origins in this idea originating on the Festiniog Railway.

History shows that the small England-designed tender tank engines of the FR quickly became less than ideal for the main line service they were required to undertake, due to the increase in traffic after they were delivered and their lack of power to haul it satisfactorily. However, their introduction was a pioneering move as, up to that date, narrow gauge steam engines had been confined to colliery, mine and factory working. Now, the FR intended to use them for powering increasing loads up its steep and sinuous main line. The engines were not really up to this and, so, during their 150 years of service to date they have seen less use in front line service than other designs subsequently utilised by the railway. Bearing this in mind, it is surprising that they continued to survive for so long. Since the railway's restoration as a tourist operation in the mid 1950s, the type has also

largely been unsuitable for the heavy tourist trains which have become the Festiniog Railway's bread and butter. Despite their undoubted historical importance and pedigree, only *Prince* has so far been restored by the railway for commercial use. Now all four survivors are regarded as 'heritage' engines, which means they recognised for their pedigree and they play a significant role in warming the market for volunteers on the railway. That is vitally important and all four still exist.

This is their story

Charles Easton Spooner, manager & clerk to the Festiniog Railway, was instructed by the board of directors in 1860 to look into the matter of providing steam engines for the railway. Local quarry magnate Samuel Holland introduced his engineer nephew Charles Holland to assist and, as Samuel was the railway's best customer, the FR could hardly refuse. Charles Holland lived in London and so wanted any engines to be built by George England at his London Hatcham Works, so that he could keep an eye on the construction. Although FR advertised for builders and received several enquiries, the railway still ordered engines from England; maybe they were

> **The introduction of steam locomotives on the FR was most likely done partly out of self defence but also with an eye to increasing traffic.**

always going to in the circumstances. Initially they only wanted one engine just to see how it worked, but England was not interested in building just one engine, so a deal was done for an initial three. The first two engines were to cost £1,000 each and the third £800. England built the engines officially to a joint design of his own and that of Charles Holland, but probably quietly suppressed some of Holland's more outlandish ideas. England knew how to build steam engines; Holland's pedigree was more doubtful.

The first two engines were delivered by July 1863. Harry and Job Williams built a large cart, hitched up four horses and went to Caernarfon to fetch the first one as it had arrived there by ship from London. Once again, the *North Wales Chronicle* takes up the story: "The long talked of and long expected steam engine for the Festiniog Railway... arrived in Port.. bedizened with evergreens and flowers as befitted the occasion, and as a matter of course created quite a sensation in the place."

James Boyd, early FR historian, well describes the engines: "These were four coupled tank engines with auxiliary tenders for carrying coal; they had inside frames and outside cylinders, whilst water

Above: *The Princess* **almost in original form (dome and cab weatherboard added) at Duffws ready to return with an early passenger train, probably in the 1870s. The current FR are gradually restoring all the original 'bug box' Brown Marshalls carriages and creating missing examples. A copy of the brake van illustrated in the picture is currently being manufacturerd at Boston Lodge.**

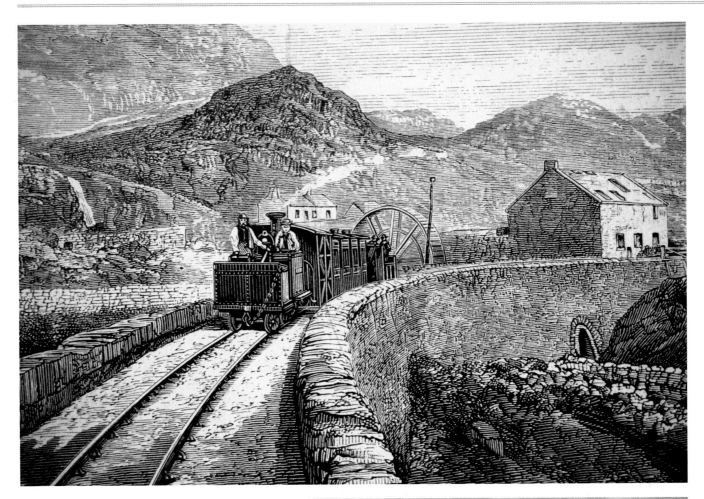

was carried in side tanks whose tops were level with the top of the boiler lagging. The chimney was bell mouthed, there was a front weather-board curved towards the top, brass dome with whistle thereon, safety valve in a brass cover on the firebox, whilst the foot-plating was curved at the front and rear."

A fourth engine was also ordered (as part of a settlement in altering the initial engines to provide domes so that they steamed properly) and, despite some confusion about which engines actually arrived in what order, the numbering settled down to be: No.1 *Princess*, No.2 *Prince*, No.3 *Mountaineer* and No.4 *Palmerston*. It is thought that *Mountaineer* may actually have arrived first and, if so, it is a pity that it is the only one of the four not to have survived in some form to the present day; it wore out and was scrapped with parts being donated to sister engines. At the time of construction, the country could talk of little else than the marriage of the Prince of Wales (to become King Edward V11) to Princess Alexandra of Denmark and, of course, Palmerston was Prime Minister, hence the engine names. Two further England engines were introduced into service in 1867, *Welsh Pony* and *Little Giant* which had several improvements built into them (including larger boilers and a longer wheelbase) which were very necessary as the original four engines proved troublesome, despite the glory and publicity of the initial public run.

The engines went through may iterations during their lives. Having been built as side tank engines with tenders, they were modified with a large weight being placed on top of their side tanks (which is often mistaken for a saddle tank) and then, at a later rebuilding, actually fitted with saddle tanks.

The engines were initially painted 'brick red'. This has often been misconstrued as a bright red colour

and, indeed, *Prince* has even been repainted as such in recent years. However, when one stops to consider the type of brick commonly used in North Wales in the mid nineteenth century, a different hue of red becomes apparent. Many buildings were constructed from Ruabon brick which was a deeper browny shade of red and, so, it is submitted that this was the more likely colour of the FR engines from the outset, as we can now see from the modern day red used on the railway.

The Princess was trialled on 4th August, 1863 and all did not go well. Charles Spooner wrote to George England about it: "Your man tried one of the locomotives today for a couple of miles... of 1 in 82 with a couple of trucks...the water flowed into the cylinders in such quantities that it was thrown out of the funnel

Above: *Welsh Pony* at **Blaenau Ffestiniog almost certainly in 'blue livery' (or what do you think?)**
Photo F.C. Carrier

Top: **Pen and ink drawing of an *England* engine on a down train between Blaenau Ffestiniog and Tanygrisiau.**

in volumes, and the injector could not work for the whole distance... the engine ran at a rate of about four miles an hour with a pressure of 60 lbs... ."

The Princess came to a complete standstill and even had to be pushed back down hill as the bearings were so stiff that she would not roll down the 1 in 82 gradient. However, most of these teething problems had been overcome by opening date and the engines were given a large dome to help overcome some of these issues. The FR opened to passenger traffic and the annual carryings of both passengers and slate increased. The Festiniog Railway was both a commercial and technical success. By 1868 (when there were six England engines in service), the company declared a half year dividend of six per cent!

But this success brought new problems. The little England engines were not now up to their task. The traffic had outgrown them. In 1869, during a Board of Trade trial, *Little Giant* was tasked with hauling a train of 51 tons: 41 slate waggons, five passenger carriages, a brake van, a rail-bending machine and Spooner's own private boat shaped inspection salon. *Little Giant* was reported to have "crept caterpillar like" up the line: "She shouldered her work in a very curious fashion. She gets over the road not steadily as she should do, but in a series of efforts rapidly repeated. As each cylinder drove the engine, so that side advanced before the other. The head of the engine sidled across the rails with a most curious crab like motion. When working hard, the engine blasted its fire to bits, giving heavy coal consumption. Wherever the track was old or rough, it was not possible to go more than about nine miles an hour at the most without incurring the risk of breaking springs or loosening the driver's teeth."

Something new in the way of steam engines for the FR was clearly needed. This was soon provided by the railway adopting the articulated Fairlie design of double engine which was heralded a great success, although both Spooner and Fairlie were publicists at large and never missed an opportunity to promote their railway and locomotive type. Cynical commentators might say that they were always on the look out for more prospects for work and loved the success of the promotion.

Once the main line traffic on the railway was in the hands of the new double engines, the England 0-4-0s became shunting engines and were held in reserve. There is little doubt that many parts were exchanged between them and, gradually, over the years in the 20th century, one by one they fell by the way side and some were simply dismantled. It is perhaps little short of amazing that four of the original six engines still survive in some form today!

Almost during their last hours, a new and additional use for some of them was found in running trains over the Welsh Highland Railway built in the 1930s to connect the North Wales Narrow Gauge Railway, which ran to the foot of Snowdon, with the Croesor Tramway running out of Porthmadoc, so joining up with the Festiniog Railway to create one large system which was even operated by the FR under lease for a while. The WHR was a tortuous railway to operate with some gradients twice as severe as the FR's and so, whilst the England engines manfully struggled on, they were not really up to the WHR task either. They served mainly to run trains from Porthmadog to Beddgelert, where passengers were then required to change to a former NWNG train for the onward journey to Dinas

> **Little Giant crept caterpillar like up the line.**

and to change, yet again, into a standard gauge LMS train to reach Caernarvon. During this time and the inter war years, several of the joint railways' coaching stock were painted into pretty unthinkable 'rainbow' colours for the tourist service and *Welsh Pony* ended up in an interesting shade of something like duck egg blue. Actually, this colour scheme has been hotly discussed and probably the better opinion is that *Welsh Pony* was really repainted green (the colour adopted at that time by Colonel Stephens who managed the railway). The latest thinking is that someone was sent from the works to buy some green paint and returned with green, but a shade which was intended for use indoors which quickly faded to a light bluey green in the sea air. Whether this is true or not probably no-one will ever know but do look at the black & white picture of *Welsh Pony* at Blaenau Ffestiniog and form your own view; the colour looks more like blue than washed out green do you not think? Anyway, we have since seen *Welsh Pony* in blue. When two Darjeeling & Himalayan Railway replica coaches were made for a private individual and painted blue, some paint was left over and, for the 50th anniversary of the railway's revival in 2005 the engine was painted in this colour which, if nothing else, set tongues wagging. Now *Welsh Pony* has been repainted green for the 150th anniversary of the England engines' introduction into service and there are more than strong rumours that restoration to steamable condition is on the cards for his own 150th birthday

Above: **Early revival years:** *Prince* **passes Boston Lodge with a train to the halt in the summer of 1955. There was no run round loop at the halt, so the carriages were run round the engine by using a chain towed by** *Prince* **to pull them round an adjacent track, the chain then being deftly unhooked to let the carriages run past the engine!**

Top: **Discarded remains of** *Little Giant* **in the long grass at Boston Lodge. If you know where to look, you can still find her driving wheels there...**

Prince with an up train near Whistling Curve on the approach to Tan-y-Bwlch station in the late 1950s. Since this picture was taken, many of the views in this woodland area have disappeared because of tree growth, but the current management has instituted a gradual clearance process which is now opening up some views through clearings.

in 2017 subject to enough sponsors being found to pay the bill.

One of the Englands, *Palmerston* was lucky enough to go on holiday several years running. The Vale of Rheidol Railway, further down the coast, asked for help with motive power, so No.4 complete with his regular driver was sent down for two separate seasons. The box insert gives a flavour of *Palmerston's* experiences...

Little Giant expired and was scrapped, or parts made available to her sisters, although her driving wheels still survive in the undergrowth in Boston Lodge's Glan-y-Mor yard if you know where to look. *Palmerston* was withdrawn and spent the remainder of his existence, before the railway closed, acting as a stationary boiler for the works' steam hammer. *Prince* was retired needing a new boiler. *Welsh Pony* simply expired in 1936. Soon it was left to *Princess* to fly the flag for the England engines and, somewhat surprisingly, she lasted right up until the end of the company's service in 1946 and even hauled the last trip freight, then retiring moribund to Boston Lodge Works to await her fate when the railway closed, although a new set of tubes were in stock but never fitted. But the type's finest hour had perhaps yet to come in the part *Prince* played in the railway's amazing and now historic revival in the 1950s under the hand of enthusiastic railwaymen who wanted to see the FR run again.

By 1955, the revivalists had managed to revive

enough of the moribund railway to contemplate operating some sort of a passenger service again. The line was being cleared and rebuilt in stages and progressively opened up to the next station along the line as resources permitted. In 1955, only the flat one mile section across the cob from Portmadoc to Boston Lodge was operable and thoughts, of course, turned to see which steam engine would be the most feasible to put back into service quickly. Attention turned straight away to *Prince* as this engine sat in the Works

Princess stands next to the weighbridge at Minffordd during the last week of operation in 1946.
Photo: Rev. Bernard Edmonds.

Palmerston's Vale of Rheidol interlude

In the summer of 1912, Army camps came to Devil's Bridge and the Territorial Army stationed at Lovesgrove. The Vale of Rheidol Railway knew that it would have to find some additional engine power and so approached the FR to see what could be available. By the end of July, *Palmerston* was on its way, couplings modified, for a month's work on the line at a hire charge of 40/- a day accompanied by his regular driver David Davies.

'Old Dafydd' wore a goatee beard and an extremely greasy bowler hat. He was so attached to 'his' engine that, reputedly, he slept in the tender to ensure that VofR men didn't get their hands on it!

When he and *Palmerston* first arrived at Devil's Bridge, his first words were "Ple mae'r inn" (where is the pub...). When asked where he had been by the Cambrian Superintendent of the line, he merely replied that he

had been listening to the birds singing in the woods...

Everything with the visit went well enough for a repeat invitation the following year for a longer visit when *Rheidol,* one of the resident engines, went away for a heavy repair. He went back again for a further three visits. Of course, not all always went well; the local crew bent a side rod on one trip and, on another, the engine left the rails completely after a disagreement with a frog on one of the sets of points at Aberystwyth. Old Dafydd's face was black as the ace of spades at this and he had tears in his eyes.

Palmerston generally acquitted himself well and was more powerful that *Rheidol,* taking three carriages and a van in dry weather. As he was different to the home fleet, he stuck in peoples' memories. Old Dafydd kept *Palmerston* lovingly polished at all times.

at Boston Lodge with a new boiler which had been ordered by the old administration and delivered but not fitted; a stroke of real luck!

Boston Lodge fitters Morris Jones and Arwyn Morgan, assisted by volunteer, laboured long and hard to get *Prince* back in steam in time for the opening, but just failed and the first world war Simplex petrol engine had to do the honours instead. Arwyn admitted later that it was all his fault as he had assembled one part the wrong way round and so the engine wouldn't move, although it was in steam for the opening day. Had he put it back the right way round, history might have been different! Nevertheless, *Prince* was soon in service and steamed across the cob on the evening of 2nd August, remarkably nine years to the very day that *Princess* had last run in the service of the old company. He faithfully hauled every passenger train for the rest of the season and also spent many evenings with working parties clearing the next section of line ahead! *Prince* was 'adopted' by the

Below: *Prince* on slate wagon empties by the weighbridge in Minffordd mineral siding in 1990. Contrast with the picture of *Princess* (opposite) in the same place.

Details of *Palmerston* restored to working order as a heritage engine.

famous (and fast) LNER driver Bill Hoole who came to the FR for an active retirement and was often seen driving him on the line. When he was 70 years old he drove 'his engine' past Boston Lodge Works serenaded by a steel band! *Prince* continued in front line service until relieved by the return of the two double Fairlies. He continued to run until 1968 before retiring as once more unsuitable for the, by now, very heavy loads of tourists requiring longer and longer trains. By this time, the FR revivalists had adopted a uniform green livery for all their engines and so *Prince* was outshopped in that colour in 1955 and looked smart too once lining had been applied.

Princess was dusted down, also repainted in green and put on exhibition at Portmadoc Harbour station and, subsequently, plinthed at Blaenau Ffestiniog in 1975 as a token gesture of faith to show that the FR meant business in reconnecting there. Once that significant milestone was achieved, *Princess* was retired first to the Harbour station museum and then ignominiously to Spooner's, the station buffet and bar!

> **❝*Palmerston* was virtually a shell by the time the revivalists arrived... one wag even renamed him Harold Wilson to update the 'England Prime Minister class'!❞**

Welsh Pony was nearly rebuilt by the revivalist regime. The tourist traffic in the late 1950s and early 1960s grew and grew until, by mid-summer, it was standing room only. Both remaining double Fairlies had re-entered traffic but *Merddin Emrys* required re-boilering and management were almost at their wits end as to how to find enough engines and carriages to meet the demand. General Manager, Alan Garraway, certainly contemplated putting *Welsh Pony* through the works as that engine was from the latter batch and slightly larger and so more powerful. But just in the nick of time, the Penrhyn Quarry Railway lent one of their main line Hunslet saddle tanks for the 1962 season, which transaction subsequently turned into a purchase of both *Linda* and her sister *Blanche*. Both Penrhyn 'Ladies' have

The hulk of *Palmerston* left to rest and rot in Glan-y-Mor yard.

Early memories...

"In my Uni holidays during the early '70s, I volunteered at Boston Lodge during the time that Paul Dukes was works manager. One day, he and I found ourselves standing next to the forlorn and dismantled parts of *Prince* and I ventured to suggest that it would be rather nice to see him working again. Paul did not speak, but his next gestures said it all. He simply dropped his fag on the floor, spat it out and twisted his foot deliberately this way and that until the fag end had disintegrated and then walked off." MW

since given sterling service to the FR and so poor old *Welsh Pony* did not get a look in and was simply stored for many years in Glan-y-Mor yard, although he did have an outing to an exhibition in Birmingham and then was subsequently plinthed for many years outside Harbour station car park as an advertisement for the railway, slowly rusting in the sea air.

Palmerston was virtually a shell by the time the revivalists arrived on the scene and they made it more so, robbing the hulk of parts to fit on *Prince*. Soon the wreck was left to rot in Glan-y-Mor and turned a horrific shade of orange with the rust. One wag even renamed him 'Harold Wilson' to update the 'England Prime Minister' class name! It seemed pretty certain that *Palmerston* would be scrapped during the 1960s as the push to rebuild the railway back to Blaenau Ffestinog was on and austerity was the name of the game. There was not any room on the locomotive roster for *Prince* so what chance *Palmerston*? However, in the nick of time a group of preservationists came along and offered to buy her. The FR has always been fortunate in that the right people come along at the eleventh hour. So, the FR sold one of its original engines for £50 with the caveat that should he ever be restored to working order then he was not to run in North Wales ever again! The FR had to eat its words, however, as *Palmerston* came into the hands of director Mike Hart who finished the restoration so that he could steam again and *Palmerston* returned to the railway to rejoin the operating fleet and still runs on occasion even in main line service, but as a member of the heritage fleet. So, miracles do sometimes happen. *Palmerston* has since been a great ambassador to the Ffestiniog Railway and has made many trips away for publicity and promotion purposes and, sometimes, simply for fun. Why not? He has even been to France!

> **A fitting touch for *Prince* to meet The Prince!**

The Opening Trip to Festiniog

"I shall now proceed to give a few details connected with this interesting event of the opening of the railway, the day being virtually kept as a holiday both at Portmadoc and Festiniog. Luckily, the day was a fine and even a brilliant one, and autumn seldom exhibited its peculiar beauties and charms more profusely or to greater advantage. Two trains started from the Portmadoc station, with an engine attached to each, the number of persons altogether being about two hundred.

The reader need not be possessed with any lively fancy to imagine to himself the laughable incidents which would be likely to occur on a line of railway when twenty carriages or so, for the first time since the creation, bounded along faster than any stage coach and with no visible propelling power; for there were hundreds of people in the neighbourhood who had never before seen a steam engine, although, of course, they had heard of one. Horses galloped about the fields like distraught animals, when the puffing engines passed along, so confused and amazed were they at the noise, and the phenomenon altogether; and the more timid cows and sheep seemed equally as astonished as were their upper-teethed and solid-hoofed friends. All along the line of rails, at every available spot, crowds of wondering people were collected in groups, from the aged crone of ninety years, to the demure little damsel of three. Here and there, the tops of the craggy hills were covered with curious and (dare we say?) gaping crowds of mountaineers, who, for the first time in their lives saw a train of carriages propelled up an incline without any horses to draw them; and to most of them, doubtless the whole affair must have been mysteriously incomprehensible. The scenery after we had left the village of Penrhyn Deudraeth, a little to the right, down in the valley, was indescribably beautiful; but about three miles from the quarries there was a tunnel over half a mile in length; and, notwithstanding the fineness of the day, riding through this subterranean passage was anything but agreeable, as the bore was then extremely small, though it has been enlarged a little since then.

When the trains' arrived at the terminus, at Blaenau Festiniog, we were greeted by hundreds of quarrymen, who were perched on the rocks many yards above us, who cheered lustily and uproariously, and as only Britons can.

The engines were piloted by Mr. Holland and Mr. England, and they must have been deeply gratified with the successful results of their skill and labour.

The scenery all along this marvellous railway is of the most grand and varied character; indeed we know of no spot in Wales which can surpass it in gorgeous and wild loveliness. The view from off the Portmadoc embankment presents one of the most extended and varied panoramic scenes in Great Britain; but the beauties which lie in the Maentwrog and Festiniog Vales cannot be perceived, nor even imagined, only from this railway. Many persons in the company, and who had resided in Portmadoc and the neighbourhood for a number of years, confessed that they had not the remotest conception of it, nor had the writer of this sketch himself. Altogether it was a natural picture which no painter could do justice to – one of nature's masterpieces, and unapproachable by art.

> **The scenery all along this marvellous railway is of the most grand character...**

Some amusing incidents took place at Festiniog on the arrival of the trains. The Blaenau juveniles thronged around the engines in the first instance; when now and again the engineers would blow the whistle to its utmost pitch, when these amazed specimens of Young Wales would scamper off at full speed, not knowing exactly what to do – laugh or scream. After a short interval, they would gradually again approach the mysterious 'animal', when another shrill blast would scatter them in all directions. A poor cow, which was in a field not far distant, was so confused and frightened that, after one of the screaming blasts, she ran over a poor sow which was grazing in the field with her, which incident caused much merriment.

In returning to Portmadoc, the engines were placed in the rear of the carriages, as they were not required until the embankment was reached, a distance of nearly thirteen miles. The speed, by gravitation alone, was from 15 to 20 miles an hour, and had the carriages been laden with slates, it would have been still greater. Crowds of people were awaiting the return, and much cheering took place. The day's proceedings terminated with a public dinner in the Town Hall, Portmadoc, Mr. George Casson occupying the chair.

Palmerston on the inaugural public passenger train run at the May 1993 gala doubleheading *David Lloyd George* across Penrhyn level crossing.

And what became of *Prince*? Well, despite there being no need for an England engine on the main line roster, it was recognised that at least one should really be working nevertheless and so *Prince* was put through the works, but rebuilt to extraordinary proportions: widened and lengthened and converted to oil firing in an endeavour to get 'the Old Gent' to pull more carriages. Whilst this mission was indeed accomplished, the serious use of *Prince* was limited to the shoulders of the seasons when the train lengths comprised the number of carriages he could manage. However, there were occasions when other main line motive power failed and at least one glorious time when *Prince* and *Palmerston* were called upon to run summer timetabled trains double headed all day as there were no other engines available!

In 2005, the 50th anniversary of the FR's revival was celebrated and *Prince* hauled the anniversary train from Porthmadog to Boston Lodge with the same two coaches as he had done back in 1955! He was also called upon to haul the Royal train on the newly reconstructed Welsh Highland Railway to Rhyd Ddu when the Prince of Wales was invited to officiate at the ceremony. A fitting touch for *Prince* to meet the Prince! Boiler certificates expire eventually and that for *Prince* was no exception. In temproary retirement he was put on display at the Severn Valley Railway's 'Engine House' but brought back to Boston Lodge for overhaul during 2012 so that he can play a leading role in the 2013 celebrations to mark the England engines' introduction into service. Remarkably, *Princess* too has been removed from the Porthmadog cafe, re-united with her tender and given a make over so she can appear in London for the first time since she was built, so as to star in her own 150th birthday. After all, a celebration without the original engine, even not in steam, would be unthinkable. Both *Princess* and *Prince* have been repainted in identical red livery, slighly lighter than the 'brick red' currently sported by *Palmerston* so as to look as cheerful as possible for the cameras - and no-one is complaining about that. Do take the chance to see the two old engines on home territory in Wales during their 150th year.

There are just two postscripts to add
We should not forget *Topsy*. Although not a two foot gauge steam engine, *Topsy* remains as originally built to remind us of what an England FR engine looked like 150 years ago. *Topsy* is a three and one eighth of an inch gauge live steam model which Charles Spooner had built in 1869 by William Williams (Boston Lodge works manager) to run in his garden just for fun in a figure of eight. Remarkably, she still survives and can be seen preserved in 'original FR brick red' livery in a glass case in Spooner's restaurant at Porthmadog Harbour station.

The very last word should probably be addressed to those leading the heritage movement at the Ffestiniog Railway. Amazingly, we have seen the whole FR main line rebuilt, the original Boston Lodge engine shed magnificently restored, nearly every surviving original carriage restored to running order and used in service, an amazing active plan for a hundred or so slate and other waggons to be returned to running order for demonstration and some bullhead rail in chairs to be restored through Minfford station. These are welcome and remarkable achievements, especially when money is often hard to come by in equipping a tourist railway. However, the four remaining 'original' England engines have not been so lucky in their place in the revival history, as has been described above. It would seem perfect if a plan could be agreed and acted upon for the survivors to have a future place alongside all these working restorations. The England engines are loved by many who would put their hands in their pockets to see them work again and the feedback during the 2013 restorations has been that there is always support for working engines, but much less so for static ones. It seems that *Welsh Pony* may be lucky but *Princess* may not. If so, she and *Livingston Thompson* would be the only FR artefacts consigned to history in static and incomplete form. Even the unique hearse van has had a couple of authentic outings. The Ffestiniog Railway prides itself in being living history. In their 150th year, this would be a great time to affirm the future of all four surviving England engines so as to match the balance of the rolling stock.

> **The England engines are loved by many who would put their hands in their pockets to see them running again.**

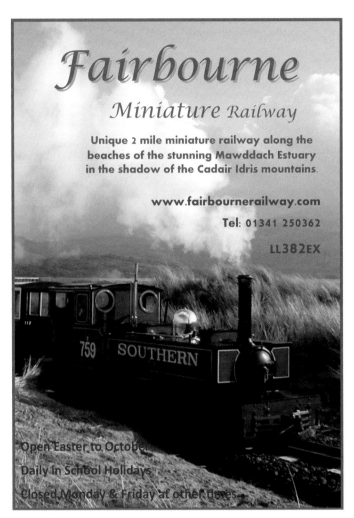

Double engines prove
TWICE
AS GOOD!

The motive power saviours of the Festiniog Railway, but not the world.

B.R. Molineux's atmospheric picture of *Merddin Emrys* blowing off waiting to leave at Portmadoc station. Still largely in original condition before rebuilding with a new parallel boiler, but featuring new stovepipe chimneys ringed with a copper cap, donated by the Summers' family, which completely transformed the locomotive's appearance. *Merddin Emrys* has now been completely rebuilt with a heritage appearance and repainted in FR maroon fully lined out. The unauthentic chimneys have been reused on a new Fairlie now named *Earl of Merioneth*; all very confusing unless you are an FR afficionado when these details are most important!

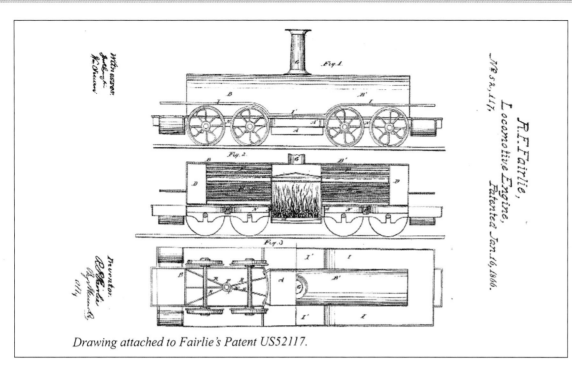

Drawing attached to Fairlie's Patent US52117.

On 6th December, 1862 Charles Holland wrote to Charles Spooner, the Festiniog Railway's manager & clerk, suggesting that the railway needed "a long centipede style of Engine on 6 or 8 wheels to creep steadily and with a great load up your line". He was right but, at that time, no one had ever built such a locomotive and so the FR started with more orthodox steam engines, as we have already discussed in an earlier essay.

Shortly after the original George England-built tender tank engines had been delivered, slate traffic boomed and the FR was carrying upwards of 100,000 tons annually, but with some difficulty as the existing engines were not built for such loads. An alternative had to be found.

Intriguingly, the solution was found by two men who were so much at loggerheads that they found themselves in court over a very emotional issue. A certain Robert Fairlie had invented a type of more powerful double engine to provide an answer for railways who faced increasing traffic but did not wish to relay their railways with heavier track or double the track. However, in a peculiar quirk of fate, he had fallen in love with Eliza, George England's daughter and, failing to get England's permission to marry her, the couple eloped and married anyway. England was furious, doubly so as Eliza was his illegitimate daughter and now his secret was out. He instigated legal proceedings against Fairlie. This could have changed the course of history for the Festiniog Railway but, fortunately, Fairlie and England were at least speaking to each other by 1868 and England, with an eye to business, expressed an interest in the double engine concept.

George England was probably the man who actually came up with the solution for the FR as he knew of its needs. Although the FR had already obtained statutory powers to double its line, England wrote to Spooner in 1868 saying: "We will undertake to make you a Fairlie double Boiler duplex Locomotive... equal in power to any two of the Engines you have now working on your line" and so he did.

The first FR double engine was aptly named *Little Wonder*. The engine was an immediate success. It ran steadily at speeds of over 30 mph; it used three quarters

A unique design...

The double Fairlie is unmistakable, a symmetrical double-ended tank locomotive fitted with a double ended boiler and carried on two power bogies fitted with conventional cylinders and motion. The distinctive boiler has a continuous water space but is fitted with two fireboxes from each of which a set of tubes extend to a smokebox at the appropriate end of the boiler. The cab is built over the central firebox casing and covers two narrow footplates on either side of the boiler. On one stands the driver, provided with a common reversing gear for both bogies but separate regulators, on the other stands the fireman who concentrates on firing the two boxes through side-mounted fire doors. On coal burning locomotives it was usual for the driver to operate the injectors leaving the fireman free to concentrate on firing and also reduce the amount of pipework on his cramped footplate. (Rodney Weaver)

of the fuel the smaller engines consumed to do the same job and caused less wear to the track. Moreover, it proved able to haul over twice as much as the existing smaller 0-4-0STTs. Whilst being a prototype, the engine certainly had its faults and soon wore out, being replaced by new and improved engines for the FR, its production and demonstration in North Wales before key international audiences probably changed the course of history

Little Wonder was an anachronistic machine, as indeed were the previous Geo. England locomotives. Her fireboxes were D shaped in plan, an obsolete form. The use of Gooch stationary link motion on a locomotive designed in 1868 was another distinctly curious feature, considering that previous FR locomotives were fitted with the superior Allan straight link motion. However, her ability to work trains of 85 tons at a average speed of 13 mph solved the FR's motive power crisis. She only lasted 13 years and probably literally shook herself to bits, although the firebox design probably did not help. The FR simply scrapped her, learned from the experience and built a successor.

Little Wonder on a publicity test train comprised of Brown Marshalls Birmingham-built low slung four wheelers (nicknamed 'bug boxes'), many of which have remarkably survived) and open top quarrymen's trucks before roofs were added.

'Valentine's commercial tinted postcard showing the second doube Fairlie *James Spooner* built by Avonside and already modified by the addition of a cab. The typical passenger train stands at Portmadoc harbour station formed of quarrymens' coach, 'bug box', two bow sider bogie carriages and a bogie van.

Livingston Thompson, built at the FR's Boston Lodge works shown in a Photocrom commercial postcard on a down train at Tan-y-Bwlch station, crossing a mixed up train. A horse and carriage waits in the car park.

facilitating the introduction of narrow gauge railways in all corners of the earth. The demonstrations also provided Fairlie with some additional sales.

Both Spooner and Fairlie were ardent publicists and took every opportunity to promote their railway and patent locomotive design so they could secure more consultancy work and sell more double engines. They arranged for an inspection and locomotive trials of the Festiniog Railway's *Little Wonder* and other Fairlie engines elsewhere by an important and influential international group of people in 1870.

A Belgian engineer of the time wrote: "recently a great noise has been made about an English line of very narrow gauge, which has been a long time at work between Festiniog and Port Madoc in Wales, but on which locomotives have only run since 1863-4. The results put forward by Mr Spooner, the directing engineer of the line, and warmly defended by R. Fairlie, certainly tend to throw a new light on the technicality of railways".

It was arranged for an inspection party of 40 or so eminent persons to visit Portmadoc. The party included the third Duke of Sutherland, a large group of Russian railway officials and engineers led by Count Alexai Bbrinskoy (who claimed descent from Catherine the Great), Captain Tyler, Carl Phil, the well known Norwegian railway engineer and officials from France, Germany and Sweden as well as the Spooners, the FR Chairman, Livingston Thompson and others.

The party started in London visiting the England/Fairlie works at Hatcham, riding a Fairlie double engine built for Sweden and a steam carriage Fairlie was promoting in the UK. On Thursday 10th February, the party then boarded special saloons attached to the 10am Scottish express. Sutherland was a director of the London & North Western Railway and also owned his own saloons, so fixing that would have been easy. At Crewe, Ramsbottom introduced the works' own 18 inch gauge railway and steel mill amongst "a mingled rattle of Russian, French, German, Scandinavian and English" conversation. Conditions for the onward journey to Portmadoc were arctic and the party had with them "a godly assortment of great coats, furs and rugs of every

Below: **Another brand new double engine built in the Boston Lodge workshop to traditional lines, although slightly larger than the original size, making this locomotive a 13in to the foot model! A new engine has a new name:** *David Lloyd George* **named after the local MP and later Prime Minister. This in turn has led FR humorists to create an FR 'dead Prime Ministers' class' for DLG and** *Palmerston!* **The new engine also has a new colour, sometimes earning it the nickname of the 'soup dragon' but we are in danger of going into rather too much modern day FR folk lore...**

shape, size and colour". The Spooners welcomed their guests on arrival and they all settled into hotels in Portmadoc and Tan-y-Bwlch before the engine trials began. Spooner laid on a demonstration of his garden model railway with Boston Lodge built miniature *Topsy* running round the figure of eight track layout in his garden and the evening being taken up by debates about the efficacy of the narrow gauge. Any narrow gauge aficionado would have given their eye teeth to be present at such discussions.

Dinner was held at 8pm on Saturday 12th February at the Tan-y-Bwlch Oakley Arms hotel with the Duke of Sutherland in the chair. Charles Spooner read his paper on the Festiniog Railway and expounded on his views of the future of the narrow gauge which he tied to the 2'6" gauge (commonly subsequently adopted in Europe), whereas Robert Fairlie proposed a three foot gauge and Norway's Carl Phil a gauge of 3'6". At least all the speakers agreed that the narrow gauge railway had a distinct and successful future. And so it proved. The golden age of the narrow gauge was dawning and the Festiniog Railway, as host, was certainly caught up in all the hype. Not that it did the railway itself much good, other than that Fairlie was so pleased with the publicity, he gave the FR perpetual royalty free rights to make double engines to his patent. Whether, because it was free we do not know, but the FR certainly went on to develop the type as its main motive power - and this remains the case even today.

The 1870 trials were certainly intended for worldwide consumption and *Little Wonder* acquitted itself well. Even the engine name was good publicity. The double engine took a load of 97 vehicles weighing 75 tons up the length of the line averaging speed of 14.5 mph to great acclaim. On the second day of the trials, one of the Geo. England 0-4-0STTs, *Mountaineer* was compared with *Little Wonder*. Almost certainly, both Spooner and Fairlie knew what the outcome would be and stage managed it but, nevertheless, the result was impressive. We have read earlier about *Little Giant* waddling along the track with pronounced horizontal oscillation. This was exaggerated by loading both her and her brother *Welsh Pony* with an 83 wagon train weighing 189 tons 13 cwt and setting off over the mile long 'Cob' only for the duo to stall just short of Minffordd. *Little Wonder* was then substituted on the same train and a complete transformation took place; she simply romped away. The double engine was stopped deliberately on Gwyndy bank, just above Minffordd station, but showed no effort or stress in restarting the train on the gradient and, indeed, accelerated to 6 mph with boiler pressure rising to 170 psi. This required a tractive effort of just over 8,000lbs and was clearly an all out effort. The trials conclusively proved that a double Fairlie engine could do more than the work of two of the England 0-4-0STTs, do it with ease and with less fuel and only one set of men as well as be kinder to the track.

An eye witness commented: "The chief point of interest in this experiment had reference to the length of the train, which was 854 ft - nearly the sixth part of a mile. A train of such length on such a line had to run often upon two or three reverse curves, some of them with a radius as short as one and three quarter chains, and it curled and doubled upon itself as it wound among the Welsh hills so that the passengers in the front carriages could, sitting in their seats, make signals to the passengers sitting in the hindmost ones. The engine being in full gear; took this very long train up the hills and in and out among the curves at an average speed of fourteen and a half miles an hour; and at a maximum speed of twenty six and a half miles an hour."

Taliesin (nee *Livingston Thompson*) outside Boston Lodge works in 1957 having been returned to service in the revival era painted green edged black.

Captain Tyler, from Her Majesty's Inspectorate of Railways was an ardent admirer and advocate of both the narrow gauge and the steam locomotive. He reported to the Board of Trade thus: "The adoption of the locomotive power upon this little line is very important, and has evidently been a very successful experiment. The cheapness with which such a line can be constructed, the quantity of work that can be economically performed upon it, and the safety with which the trains run over it, render it an example which will, undoubtedly, be followed sooner or later in this country, in India, and in the colonies, where it is desirable to form cheap lines for small traffic, or as a commencement in developing the resources of a new country". A most prophetic statement.

Early memories...

"It was always irritating to me as a child to be presented with choices when I wanted to do both options. Such was the case when *Taliesin* (nee 'LT') was due to be renamed *Earl of Merioneth*. We were in Wales for the occasion and it transpired that *Merddin Emrys* was also undergoing trials on the very same day. I had managed to take a satisfactory box camera photograph of the latter at Portmadoc, but wanted to follow him up the line to take more, when PBW announced that we were going to *Taliesin*'s renaming at Tan-y-Bwlch. But, as luck would have it, I got the last laugh as both engines appeared there double heading the train for the renaming and so I got my additional photographs and PBW attended the renaming, which I regarded as a bit of a damp squib and something that shouldn't be done; once an engine had a name it should keep it." MW

Classic FR double engine lines shown by *Earl of Merioneth* (nee *Taliesin*, nee *Livingston Thompson*) taking water at Portmadoc station at Easter in April 1969; the locomotive was still then in original FR form, unaltered or modified in any way.

Old or new engines and both double Fairlies? The engine on the left is indeed a double fairlie, the rebuilt *Merddin Emrys*, but the engine on the right is a brand new single Fairlie *Taliesin* built at a cost of £200,000 by monthly subscribers who yearned to complete the FR's missing locomotive type. Are you confused by all the engine name changes yet?

So, the trials had achieved Fairlie's objective. His patent locomotive was adopted for a narrow gauge line in Russia and other orders started to flow in. The Festiniog went on to commission a further double engine, *James Spooner* from Avonside and then, subsequently, to build two of its own: *Merddin Emrys* and *Livingston Thompson* both of which are still with us, or at least the nameplates and some parts are. The FR has always been in the habit of rebuilding anew when needed. Indeed, the Boston Lodge official records say of the reboilering of *James Spooner* in 1904-8 "old engine condemned and cut up". This practice continues today. After the restoration, it was found that both the surviving Boston Lodge Fairlies had poor boilers and, recognising that they were going to be heavily needed once the line was rebuilt to Blaenau Ffestiniog, took the bold step to make two new boilers. Indeed, the repairs required to *Livingston Thompson* (by then renamed *Earl of Merioneth*) were so extensive that the railway decided to build a completely new engine. It was only the remonstrations of an 'active forty' group of volunteers which got the superstructure saved, placed on old bogies and lent to the National Railway Museum for display. Subsequently, even another brand new double Fairlie has been built by the railway in the restoration years *David Lloyd George* and, at the time of writing, a whole new series of bogies are under construction with piston valves to increase efficiency and

> **"The golden age of the narrow gauge railway was dawning."**

lessen wear and tear. Now no-one can contemplate the Ffestiniog Railway without Fairlie's double engines: the two are almost synonymous. Every visitor who goes to the Ffestiniog Railway should be guaranteed to see one of the type in action and be able to ride behind it. The double Fairlie locomotive is now unique to that railway.

Whilst several railways did indeed order and use Fairlie double engines, the type never became the dominant motive power for developing countries as perhaps Fairlie had hoped and planned; certainly the Beyer Garratt type (as we will see later) came to be much more respected and useful and was probably the most successful type of articulated engine to have been produced. Nevertheless, Fairlie sold many of his type of patent engine, although whether this was due to excellence of design or persuasion and relationships must be open to some doubt.

Fairlie was a profound and prolific influencer of journalists who probably also stood to gain from promoting the double engine and he also seemed to be able to install friendly engineers on the foreign railways which purchased his engines. One engineer who certainly did not believe the Fairlie hype was one W.W. Evans who wrote one of the most vitriolic condemnations of the double engine type and its inventor found published to date. Of the sales of the patented engine to Chile's Iquique Railway he wrote: "Mr Fairlie had won the affections of the Brothers Montero, the owners of the Iquique Railway and by some 'hocus pocus' had made them believe that the engine he called his was something wonderful and destined to regenerate the railway world. The Monteros were 'innocents' and allowed their money bags to flow freely into the pockets of Fairlie. A merchant in Lima said the Fairlie engines were the best he ever heard of, because they ruined the rails, they ruined themselves, and the more they got the more they wanted, and the more they ordered the more his commissions were... An eminent German railway manager says he has no engines on his line that cost as little for repairs as Fairlies, for he takes good care never to use them".

As they say, life has swings and roundabouts. What was good for the Ffestiniog 'goose' was not necessarily also good for the foreign railway 'gander'. Enter Herbert William Garratt.

The revival era built a brand new double engine to replace *Earl of Merioneth* and transfered the nameplates but also used both bogies and several other parts from the withdrawn original engine which was planned to be scrapped. This caused consternation with some of the volunteers resulting in a group self titled the 'Active Forty' raising cash to ensure the withdrawn engine was retained for display. Here we see the new double engine crossing the high stone wall Cei Mawr embankment with the Editor and family dog leaning out of the front window. The utilitarian lines of the new engine quickly earned it the nickname of 'The Square'! The headboard celebrates the 150th anniversary of the Festiniog Railway Company. Photo: Hugh Ballantyne.

K1

The World's first Garratt articulated steam locomotive

K1's story is extraordinary. It is little short of miraculous that she still survives today and in working order as well. This is her story.

Herbert William Garratt served an apprenticeship with the North London Railway and then held various short term contracts with foreign railways such as the Central Argentine Railway, Cuban Central Railways and the Lagos Government Railway. During this time he gained much experience of operating steam engines in difficult conditions: severe track curvature, steep gradients, weak bridges and haulage of trains with underpowered locomotives. His inventive mind led him to devise a novel but entirely pragmatic solution for an articulated locomotive which he patented in 1908.

He conceived an engine which looked like no other but which was to be manufactured in great quantity in Manchester by Beyer, Peacock & Co and exported all over the world. So successful was the locomotive type that many hundreds were built.

Garratt only used conventional engineering thinking but turned the output of that on its head to secure a very satisfactory option to solve the need for larger and more effective motive power in the British colonies. He designed an engine with a large but short boiler mounted on its own frame with a driving cab at one end with two engines placed at either end on top of which were placed the fuel and water. The outputs of this extraordinary appearance were simple and effective: a large boiler with wide firebox and short but multiple tubes for good steaming, a low slung boiler to provide the driver with the best possible view of the line ahead, a low axle load for light track and an ability to run in either direction without the need to turn or with any inconvenience. Having created this novel design he then had to interest a manufacturer.

After a few false starts he fell in with the famous locomotive builder Beyer, Peacock in a stroke of luck. At the turn of the nineteenth century, this firm had re-organised and was considering how best to provide for

K1 in action near the Montezuma falls on the North East Dundas Tramway in Tasmania.
[Photo: H.J.King]

Left: **K1 in service on the Welsh Highland Railway, rounding the horseshoe curve immediately before Rhyd Ddu station. Mission accomplished!**

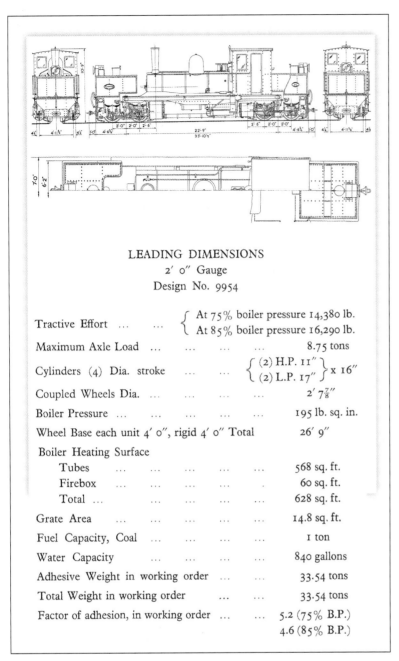

LEADING DIMENSIONS
2' 0" Gauge
Design No. 9954

Tractive Effort	At 75% boiler pressure 14,380 lb. / At 85% boiler pressure 16,290 lb.
Maximum Axle Load	8.75 tons
Cylinders (4) Dia. stroke	(2) H.P. 11" / (2) L.P. 17" } x 16"
Coupled Wheels Dia.	2' 7⅞"
Boiler Pressure	195 lb. sq. in.
Wheel Base each unit 4' 0", rigid 4' 0" Total	26' 9"
Boiler Heating Surface	
Tubes	568 sq. ft.
Firebox	60 sq. ft.
Total	628 sq. ft.
Grate Area	14.8 sq. ft.
Fuel Capacity, Coal	1 ton
Water Capacity	840 gallons
Adhesive Weight in working order	33.54 tons
Total Weight in working order	33.54 tons
Factor of adhesion, in working order	5.2 (75% B.P.) / 4.6 (85% B.P.)

K1's outline drawing and leading dimensions.

its own future. Its directors reflected on how to grapple with the changes of the times: more competition in locomotive manufacture, electrification of tramways for which the firm had build many steam trams and the beginning of road competition. One answer was to continue to produce steam railway locomotives so as to make the best use of existing plant and capital investment but to make much larger steam locomotives so as to haul greater amounts of traffic. Garratt had appeared on the scene at the right time and fortuitously struck up a friendship with Beyer's Works manager, Samuel Jackson, who could see that this new articulated type would be a winner and so helped design the patent type into workable and saleable proposition.

At this time the North East Dundas Tramway in far away Tasmania were looking for new and more powerful locomotives for their two foot gauge railway. England could hardly have been further away but, nevertheless, an enquiry came in for articulated steam railway locomotives to replace their existing fleet. They

> **Garratt's inventive mind led him to devise a novel but entirely pragmatic solution for an articulated locomotive.**

were sent a scheme for a Garratt type. The response came back that they wanted a compound engine, so the scheme was modified and resubmitted. This had the desired effect and the first Garratt was ordered on 28th January, 1909 closely followed by an order for a second on 12th March: K1 and K2 were set out in the Manchester works and history was made. Both engines were shipped on 7th October, 1909 and the Garratt type subsequently became the mainstay of production at Beyer, Peacock with examples being shipped all over the world.

Meanwhile both K1 and K2 remained in service in Tasmania until the tramway closed in 1930. Amazingly, rather than be scrapped, the engines survived and Beyer, Peacock repatriated one of the locomotives for preservation at their works in 1947. Supposedly this was K1 but we now know that it was actually an amalgamation of the best parts of both K1 and K2, but called K1.

When Beyer, Peacock's works closed in 1966 a new home was sought for K1. Initially there were no takers as

narrow gauge preservation was still then in its infancy and all efforts and cash were being put in to revive some of the Welsh narrow gauge lines for tourism. However, Bill Broadbent, then Chairman of the Festiniog Railway Society, which supported the world famous Festiniog Railway, clinched a deal which saw the FRS buy K1 for £1,000 and have it delivered to Portmadoc Harbour station. Despite the agreed undoubted historical pedigree of K1, there was considerable disquiet amongst the FR people at this purchase as they could see no use for the engine as it was far too big for the FR loading gauge and, as always, money could have been better spent on other things. Nevertheless, Broadbent was unrepentant and K1 duly went on display at Harbour station causing considerable interest. The Festiniog Railway's house magazine had this to say about it: "The Garratt is, of course, not 'train ready'. She weighs 34 tons, is (as usual)

too high, needs firebox attention and there is a suspicion that her low-pressure cylinders will fit some of our narrower clearances like wheat in a sack; but she is the *Little Wonder* of her type and posterity should judge her, as we do, a unique and wholly appropriate acquisition".

Traffic demands were growing on the FR in the 1960s and there was a dire need for more engines with increased haulage capacity. Paul Dukes, the FR Works Manager drew up a scheme to alter K1 to fit the FR loading gauge and so become a useful engine. This would have meant drastic alterations: moving the cylinders inwards and significantly reducing the height of the locomotive. Although Paul would doubtless have attacked this conversion with glee, historical common sense prevailed and the engine was sent on loan to the National Railway Museum for the indefinite future where it appeared in works

K1 on display at Porthmadog harbour station in 1966 shortly after arrival from Beyer, Peacock's Gorton Works.

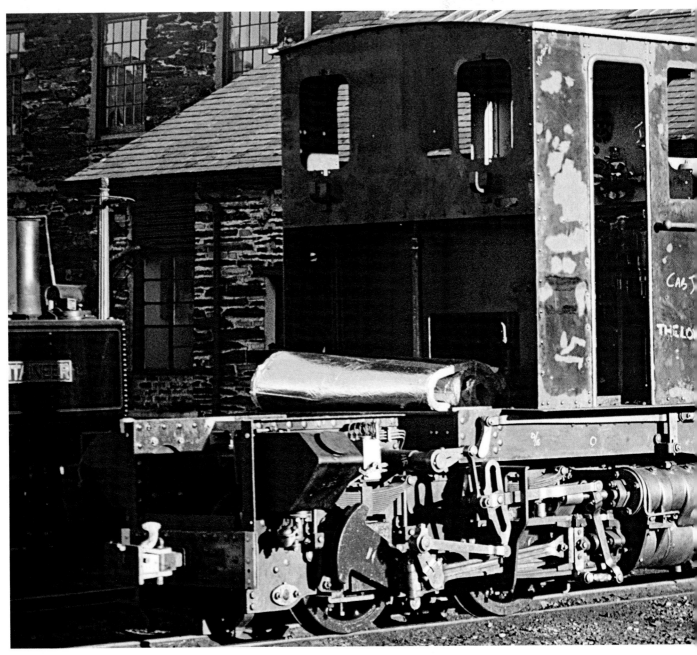

grey livery. And that is undoubtedly where K1 would have ended up were it not for the reconstruction of the Welsh Highland Railway by the FR, so adding more improbable facts to K1's life.

The Welsh Highland Railway was originally connected to the FR and the loading gauge was very similar. However, when it came to be reconstructed from dereliction by the FR the rebuilding scheme was different to the original. The promoters could see that the rejuvenated line would be very popular with tourists as it ran through wild undeveloped mountain scenery. Its steep gradients and sharp reverse curves would be a hindrance to smaller

engines trying to haul long trains. So, the idea was born to use Garratt locomotives as, fortunately, a supply of the last type ever built for the two foot gauge, NGG16 2-6-2+2-6-2 had become available from South Africa, including the last Garratt ever manufactured by Beyer, Peacock at its Manchester Gorton Works. An initial three were purchased and restored and set to work on the WHR as it was rebuilt. This set some of the promoters thinking. Wouldn't it be nice to remove K1 from the National Railway Museum at York, rebuild it and set her to work on the WHR so that the railway could demonstrate the very first and the very last Garratt engines working together? Of course it would! But the budget for the rebuilding of the WHR was a challenge enough to raise as it was, without stretching to the repair of K1.

A compromise was reached in that K1 would be rebuilt away from the WHR by a separate team of volunteers who would raise all the necessary finance independently but with the understanding that the engine would have its home on the Welsh Highland Railway and see service there within its operational limits (it is smaller than an NGG16 and so would not be able to haul the heaviest of trains in future years

Early memories...

"When I became involved with the recreation of the WHR project, it immediately occurred to me that there was only one locomotive which was a must have for the line: K1. I suggested this to the FR board and was told that they would agree my proposal but I would have to arrange to source all the labour and funds as none could be diverted from the immediate task of rebuilding the railway. I agreed and did." MW

> The Garratt type subsequently became the mainstay of production at Beyer, Peacock with examples being shipped all over the world.

once the line was fully rebuilt and extended right back to Porthmadog).

So, K1 was extracted from the NRM and taken by road to Tyseley Locomotive Works in Birmingham, a central location with all the requisite equipment and knowledge to help the embryo restoration team led by Welsh Highland Railway Society member Colin Hill. Here K1 was stripped for assessment and repair and all the difficult issues uncovered. It had been determined to restore K1 to working order whatever the ultimate cost and whatever needed doing to achieve this aim. Always a potentially controversial decision when a unique pioneer historical artifact is concerned, but that was the decision made and the team set about undertaking all the necessary repairs, including the provision of a brand new boiler. Of course, the restoration cost and time escalated but more money was found and more effort expended. Eventually, K1 steamed for the first time in the Boston Lodge workshop of the Ffestiniog Railway on 12th

September, 2004: a further historical milestone had been achieved: K1 was back in working order.

She was taken by road to The WHR's Dinas depot outside Caernarfon for final remedial works and trials and ran her first WHR train from Caernarfon to Rhyd Dddu for members of the supporting fundraising group sporting both Welsh and Tasmanian flags: K1 was back in revenue earning service and the mission had been achieved.

Despite her relatively small size, K1 has put in some sterling performances on the WHR, even hauling as many as ten coaches on the first section to Rhyd Ddu for a visiting group. Her haulage capacity is not sufficient for every day use in passenger service, so the K1 restoration team have undertaken to look after her again at no cost to the F&WHR, so that she can be seen in occasional use in anger when circumstances permit. K1 remains the only working compound Garratt steam locomotive in the world and justifies her place on the F&WHR locomotive roster simply because of that.

A 1930s
'FAERY LAND'
WELSH NARROW-GAUGE TRAIN JOURNEY

By 1930 the end was in sight. One of England's narrow-gauge lines, the Southwold, had closed in 1929; not yet having lost any money but having seen the writing on the wall, and the other railways which had not been included in the 1923 Grouping were far from happy. The situation was temporarily saved in Ireland for there the roads in the remoter districts served by the narrow-gauge were still poor. During the summer of 1933 an enthusiastic schoolboy, believing that the narrow-gauge was to the mountains of North

Right: **"The 0-6-4T *Moel Tryfan* backed out of her corrugated iron shed her cylinder cocks open and yellow smoke oozing from her stove pipe chimney."**

Below: **"The train headed by an LNWR 'Cauliflower' disgorged her passengers across the platform to pack the sagging coaches of the Welsh Highland train."**

Narrow Gauge Steam

Wales what the standard gauge was to the rest of the country, talked his parents into allowing him to make his first solo train journey. Part of it was over the greatest white elephant of all: the Welsh Highland.

At this time the posters around the North Wales resorts were advertising a trip through 'Faery Land' using the metals of the LMS, the Festiniog and the Welsh Highland Railways. After much timetable study (for the Welsh Highland service in particular was very meagre) it was found that the 11.30 am from Bangor to Afon Wen could begin the journey. The train of eight full bogies was headed by an ex-LNWR 'Cauliflower' 0-6-0, and by midday she had blasted her throaty way up to Dinas Junction and disgorged her passengers across the platform to pack the sagging coaches of the Welsh Highland train. Beyond the platform line, the 0-6-4T *Moel Tryfan* backed out of her corrugated iron shed, her cylinder cocks open and yellow smoke oozing from her stove pipe chimney. With a clang and a jar she

joined her train, raising cries of mock alarm from her indulgent passengers, at 12.38 the aged guard signaled the right away. *Moel Tryfan*, slipping and hissing on her protesting way, climbed past the shed on the right with *Russell* standing forlornly outside, rounded the long curved cutting and set course for Waenfawr. The rainbow painted coaches, the guard climbing along the running boards with a rack of bus type tickets as his only uniform, and the grass grown track proclaimed no main line, but one on its last legs; so the schoolboy glued his eyes and ears to what mattered. Occupancy of a corner seat granted him an ecstacy of whirling rods as *Moel Tryfan* plodded on up the impressive climb past Quellyn Lake to South Snowdon. Here most passengers disembarked to investigate a commotions which had appeared at the rear end; a resistant knot was undone, a two-stroke motor broke into life, the P.W. gang of semi-centenarians climbed into position and chugged sideways down the hill so laboriously climbed by *Moel Tryfan*. The Col. Stephens trolley

"Here most passengers disembarked to investigate a commotion which had appeared at the rear end; a resistant knot was undone, a two-stroke motor broke into life, the P.W gang of semi-centenarians climbed into position and chugged sideways down the hill."

"The LMS men holding the Llandudno Junction connection at Blaenau were not amused and barely waited for the passengers to join it."

disappeared round the bend to a derisive chorus from the gallery.

At Beddgelert there was a six minute wait whilst the fire was cleaned, and here the schoolboy managed to talk the crew into allowing him a footplate ride for the remainder of the journey. It was said once that a special race of dwarfs was bred to man the Welsh narrow gauge engines and the schoolboy, comparatively tall, found his hair giving the cab roof such a cleaning as it never had for years. *Moel Tryfan* leaked steam and smoke from everywhere and outside it was raining so hard so there was not much scenery to see, but the 0-6-4T's unpredictable acceleration after descending through the Aberglaslyn Pass and the Nantmor tunnel busily sped her train along the four straight and level miles into Portmadoc.

Then followed a depressing walk across the GWR and through the dripping wet town for a quick lunch, in time to see the Festiniog double engine *Merddin Emrys* appear out of the driving mist and back onto her train. At Minffordd a party of campers took possession of the train and followed one another out of the windows of the locked doors, over the roof and into the windows on the other

Merddin Emrys at Portmadoc waiting to take PBW's train up to connect with the LMS at Blaenau Ffestiniog.

> ❝ ... a man in the compartment asked the schoolboy what he had been doing and had he looked in the mirror lately? ... it took three days to get the soot and grease from his hair ... ❞

side, much to the dismay and consternation of the elderly guard, who feared for the consequences if this were attempted again whilst the train was moving. *Merddin Emrys* slipped violently and lost time all the way to Blaenau, the steam leaking from her joints combining effectively to block out any sight of the Vale of Ffestiniog, and making the passage of the Moelwyn tunnel an experience not to be voluntarily repeated. The LMS men holding the Llandudno Junction connection at Blaaenau were not amused and barely waited for the passengers to join it. On the return run in the main line train, a man in the compartment asked the schoolboy what he had been doing and had he looked in the mirror lately? He did his best with all the towels and soap he found in the toilet, for fortunately it was a corridor coach, but the arrival back at the hotel did not produce a great welcome – it took three days to get the soot and grease from his hair and the hotel pillow cases suffered accordingly. It was certainly a good day out. **PBW**

We never closed
The Story of the rescue of the Talyllyn Railway

Towyn. Off by the Toy Railway

In high summer, four carriages and a van were insufficient to carry all the traffic on offer, so slate wagons were simply added to the train for passengers to sit in. There were no continuous brakes anyway. Families could hire a slate wagon, have it towed up the line behind a train and gravitate back to Towyn at their leisure after the last train had run.

After the Second World War, several railway enthusiasts could see that railways in Britain would never be the same again and wanted to do something to keep part of the past alive. As many of them had actively participated in fighting for their nation, peace and democracy, they were more than keen to create some tranquility. War results in change and development of technology. The development of the diesel engine and the significant advances being made in road transportation would mean drastic changes for Britain's railways and almost certain death for most of the smaller narrow gauge by-lines. Could one of them be saved? Nothing like that had ever been thought about in Britain before, although in the USA there had been an abortive attempt to save the two foot Bridgetown & Harrison Railroad in Maine.

Eyes first went to the famous Festiniog Railway in North Wales, but this was moribund, overgrown

The 'Old Lady' stands at Towyn Wharf station with the first train of the preservation era on 14th May, 1951. Tom Rolt wears a panama hat alongside the first coach. Bill Trinder chats to a member by the side of *Dolgoch*. There are some 25 people in the picture; not a lot for one of the most momentous occasions in the World's railway history: the takeover of a statutory railway company by volunteers.

A John Adams classic back & white shot of *Talyllyn* storming away from Dolgoch station for publicity purpose. John was a professional photographer and part of the Adams & Whitehouse 'Railway Roundabout' team and later he went on to be Chairman and President of the TRPS.
Photo; John Adams

and appeared to be tangled up with insoluble legal difficulties. So attention began to search for another, more feasible, proposition to save.

A few miles down the Welsh coast there still operated a smaller narrow gauge mineral railway built to carry slate from the Bryn Eglwys quarry, nestling in the foothills of Wales' Cader Idris mountain, down to the Cambrian Railway at Towyn in the middle of Cardigan Bay: The Talyllyn Railway, named after a rather dour mountain lake higher up in the mountain range.

The Talyllyn Railway was still running: just. Remarkably, it was still running with all its original 1865 equipment still intact. The original two steam locomotives, built on the edge of the English Lake District by Fletcher Jennings at Whitehaven and sailed down the coast to begin their long and faithful working lives, were still extant and one, *Dolgoch*, named after a hamlet with scenic waterfalls, still hauled the thrice weekly passenger service, albeit only just. The five original carriages built by Brown Marshalls in

Birmingham (one even being first class) still provided transport for locals to Towyn's Friday market and for holiday makers in summer. The track and engineering facilities were pretty much original too and most of that had worn completely so that the rails were often held together simply by the grass which grew between them.

Unfortunately the reason for the railway being there in the first place had ceased to exist. The quarry had closed. But the railway still clung to life precariously as it's owner declared that it would continue to do so during the rest of his life and he paid all the expenses from his own pocket which the railway could not cover from the meagre revenue. The owner was Sir Hadyn Jones, MP for Merionethshire; a patron to his cause of representing his people. He died in 1950 and the general manager, Edward Thomas, who had run the railway

Above: **The early days of the TR. No. I** *Talyllyn*, **the engine crew's favourite, stands at Dolgoch station taking on water whilst the passengers detrain to watch. From here, there are idyllic walks to three levels of water falls and a hotel down by the road serving afternoon tea.**

Corris No. 4 helps out the 'Old Lady' at last, even though repairs are not quite finished. Here we see probably the first TR double header in history about to leave Towyn Wharf station on 2nd June, 1952 with the first train of the season and almost certainly No. 4's inaugural TR passenger run. The train is formed of the entire coaching stock on the railway.

The TR brake van had a ticket window in one side for use at the various stations and halts on the line, none of which were manned. Here we see Dorothy Boyd and her two children pretending to buy tickets for the camera. In reality, she would have had a free pass.

engine, *Dolgoch*, had succumbed to a broken spring and was incapacitated. Undaunted, Tom walked the track up the beautiful Fathew Valley and was immediately hooked. He wrote to the *Birmingham Post* newspaper and called a public meeting in that City's Imperial Hotel to discuss what could be done to save the Talyllyn Railway for posterity, fortunately without thought to all the considerable problems and cost which could lie ahead...

The meeting was a resounding success. It resulted in the formation of the Talyllyn Railway Preservation Society run by amateur enthusiasts who managed to persuade Sir Haydn's widow to give them the railway! She did this by allowing the TRPS to have a majority shareholding in the statutory Talyllyn Railway Company but also retaining a seat on the board of directors. To this day there is still a director nominated by the descendants of Haydn Jones!

So what did the pioneers of railway preservation find when they took over the service for the 1951

Above: **Corris No. 3 (with No. 4 in the background) with a team of inspectors when the engines were in store at Machynlleth. British Rail sold them to the TR for £25 each. Luckily they were the same gauge and literally only just down the road.**

for years, knew that at the end of the season he would have to close and lock the booking office door finally for the last time. The Talyllyn Railway would expire and crumble to rust.

Almost at the last hour, now famous canal and industrial archaeological historian and writer, Tom Rolt, stumbled across the Talyllyn Railway for the first time, sadly on a day when the only working steam season? They found a railway which should, in all reality, have been closed and dismantled many years before, but they set to and, over the next fifty years, achieved the impossible: a triumph of enthusiasm over logic.

The boiler inspector came to assess whether *Dolgoch* remained fit to run. Repairs had been made to the boiler in the 1940s but that was some time ago. The inspector insisted that a sample hole was drilled in the boiler to assess its thickness and so its suitability for service. Fortunately, the test was positive and so the grand 'Old Lady' served for the first season. Interestingly, when she was later taken out of service for rebuilding with a new boiler it was found that the thickness of the boiler plates either side of the test drill hole was little more than an eight of an inch! Had the inspector drilled a few inches to the right or the left, the outcome and future of the railway might have been very different...

Everything was worn out, so nothing was easy for the first season. Indeed the track was so bad that even the Preservation Society felt that they should restrict initial services to just the first station for the re-opening in May 1951, until they had made sure the rails up the line were more or less to gauge and held fast in the chairs and sleepers. Originally, the rails were simply laid end to end with the join between sections clamped together by metal chairs pinned to wooden sleepers. As the joints wore through the years, the track easily became dislodged causing derailments. Reluctantly, the previous owners had hired a local man painstakingly to drill each rail end and fit the rails with fishplates so they were bolted together to keep in gauge. However, he never finished his task and the early preservation journeys up the line had the driver facing the alarming prospect of *Dolgoch* placing her wheels on one end of the rail which caused the other end to rise up out of the chair clasp, only to settle back again as the train advanced up the track. Hair raising!

But the train service never completely stopped. Yes there were days when trains couldn't run as some defect or other was being fixed, but the timetable was always posted. Even the May 1951 're-opening' was really misnomer as the timetable was only suspended over the preceding winter for not many tourists brave the Welsh winter.

Clearly the original equipment was not going to continue to serve the railway well without much care, attention and cash being spent to refurbish it completely. Alternatives had to be found to keep the trains running and, also, more carriages were needed as publicity about the new enterprise resulted in a dramatic increase in traffic: two fold, three fold and more over the next ten years. The TR clearly had a guardian angel for the right help was at hand at the right time. Several Society members gave freely of their time and their business facilities. Amazingly, in just the next valley south from the TR there used to be a similar narrow gauge railway even having the same track gauge: the Corris Railway. Even more amazingly, two of its steam engines had survived in store at the nearby railhead at Machynlleth. Negotiations saw them acquired at £25 each: a bargain even in the 1950s. Appropriately, they were given the names *Sir Haydn* and *Edward Thomas* after the two people who perhaps put more time and effort into ensuring the TR survived until preservation times. They kept their original Corris Railway numbers: Nos. 3 and 4 respectively.

Left: **"Dolgoch"** at Dolgoch in the first year of TRPS operation during 1951 with Tom Rolt as guard

Below: **Douglas Ableson holding the nameplate for the yet to be restored No. 6 Andrew Barclay 0-4-0WT at the handover ceremony, watched by Pat Whitehouse (in the cab) and The Earl of Northesk in the pin striped suit.**

No. 7 *Tom Rolt* at Wharf on 7th May, 2001. This is ostensibly a new engine using redesigned parts from an Irish Andrew Barclay which chief engineer, John Bate, nicely made suit the profile of the new carriages. Here we see a completely modern TR scene; everything is new to the railway, apart from the original station building partly obscured by the platform canopy.

Above: **'Peter Sam' on holiday from the Skarloey Railway, crossing Dolgoch viaduct. The Rev W. Awdry based his books on engine characters and events on the Talyllyn Railway which proved a real publicity boost and 'Peter Sam' was such a nice friendly engine too.**

Left: **The mineral extension in the late 1960s, showing the trackbed in the condition the whole railway was in at preservation.**

No. 2 *Dolgoch* clearly was not going to be able to soldier on for very much longer; some might say she was well past it already. So, efforts were made to ready Corris No. 3 to working order as quickly as possible as initial inspections showed that she would be the quickest engine to put back into working order. But the engineers had reckoned without the diabolical state of the Talyllyn track. When No. 3 ran her first trips, she continually fell between the rails as the track gauge varied as much as half an inch. She would have to have her wheels retyred before she would be of any reliable use. This left No. 4 which required considerably more work, but the engineering team set to with some external help from well wishers who, as often happened with the TR,

came upon the railway at the right time. No. 4's wheel tyres were more forgiving and so, when he returned to steam, success was on hand and *Dolgoch* could be semi-retired. Additionally, a third engine had been given to the TR on condition it was named 'Douglas' after the donor, a condition gladly accepted. It was an Andrew Barclay 0-4-0WT from the RAF and had to be regauged from her two foot to fit on the TR's 2'3" track, a job undertaken by Hunt Brothers foundry in the Midlands. With almost a surfeit of working steam

TALYLLYN RAILWAY PRESERVATION SOCIETY

This is to certify that

P. B. WHITEHOUSE ESQ.

is recorded as a Life Member of the Talyllyn Railway Preservation Society

Date 25/6/53. Issued by

Signature of Holder

If this card is lost advise the Secretary immediately quoting the number : L 65

engines, the original two locomotives could be sent away for a thorough rebuilding at the Midlands works of a donor member, Eric Gibbons, who volunteered to restore the engines at no cost to the railway. Indeed, the rebuildings were so severe that very little remained of the original locomotives. A shame that replicas were not built and the original two engines gracefully retired to a museum, but that was not the thinking in the 1950s.

The endemic problem with preserving a railway is that such objectivity is not possible if it is to function as a working railway. Virtually everything on the TR had to be repaired, restored if not completely renewed. Furthermore, the success and publicity of volunteers running a public railway for the first time, aided and abbetted by an expanding caravan holiday industry by the Welsh sea and a very successful BBC TV live outside broadcast show in 1957, led to record crowds. This required more carriages, more engines, additional passing loops to enable more trains to be run on the single line and the addition of catering facilities and more sheds to keep everything in. This resulted in the TR carrying many times more than its intended original passenger capacity as more and more people flocked to the line. Whilst everyone - passengers and volunteers alike - were having a whale of a time, the Talyllyn Railway was gradually looking less and less like it had ever done before. Whilst the rebuilding and expansion meant that it could cope with all these additional demands, it could be said that it was becoming the least preserved railway as well as being the first preserved railway. The Talyllyn Railway would, of course, be the first to deny that as it still sports its 'original' train running up the original route; and that is true. But, apart from some of the wayside stations, the railway's ancient and ramshackle ambience has been lost for ever in the name of preservation progress.

And ironically, in the 21st Century, passenger traffic levels have fallen alarmingly but interestingly almost back to the pre-war levels when it ran as a slate carrier but with summer holiday traffic. Why? Because the caravanners and holiday makers who used to frequent the many bed & breakfast hotels in the area have now deserted Wales for warmer climes in Spain and a much fewer number now come to stay in the region. This is a great pity for the TR is now in probably the best condition it has ever been with a thriving volunteer team and has built many superb new coaches for its service and even an almost new engine which it acquired from Ireland and named *Tom Rolt* after the line's saviour. Maybe some adjustments can be made to show a little more of the ambience of the original railway

and re-consider how it is promoted, probably in conjunction with the local community to seek to encourage more visitors to this very beautiful part of Wales.

The preservation regime has introduced many significant improvements. A superb railway museum of narrow gauge railways can now be found at the Tywyn Wharf station, featuring many artefacts and locomotives rescued from the scrap heap. A thriving cafe and well stocked souvenir shop also at Wharf and a simple, but equally pleasant, cafe at Abergynolwyn, the original passenger terminus station frequented by all trains. From here the line continued towards the slate quarry, reached by two inclined planes. The preservation society rebuilt this mineral extension to the foot of the first incline and created a new station, Nant Gwernol, in idyllic surroundings above a river ravine coupled with several lovely mountain walks. It is quite possible to spend a super day in the area by taking a train to Nant Gwernol, walking around the ravine and the old mineral inclines and back to either Abergynolwyn or Dolgoch Falls station and then taking the train back dow the Afon Fathew valley. Then railway promotes this concept well, but it would be good for the future of the line and the locality if more people came to enjoy this facility and this remains the Talyllyn Railway's challenge.

Below: **"We are having a lovely holiday here in Towyn"**, so reads the reverse of this Frith commercial postcard showing *Talyllyn* on a down mixed train with loaded wooden slate wagons following the Birmingham-built Brown Marshalls carriages.

Cat-y-Elyn Railway, Towyn

Dolgoch
The 'Old Lady'

Above: **John Adams' classic shot of the 'Old Lady'. *Dolgoch* at Rhydyronen station in the very early years of the preservation society; nothing has yet changed and so 'preservation' in the title of the society was apt.**

The 1865 built 0-4-0WT *Dolgoch* is synonymous with the Talyllyn Railway. Neither would be there without the other and the preservation regime would not have had the faintest hope of success if she had not survived the 1951 season, which she did against all odds and logic.

Neither *Dolgoch* or her sister *Talyllyn* were the first of a line, or unique, or trend setting as, say the Festiniog Railway England engines discussed elsewhere in this publication. Yet, they were both built at a time when steam narrow gauge engines were still in their infancy during the cradle of steam locomotive development.

Both engines were ordered by the Aberdovey Slate Co. Neither engine was designed as a passenger engine, but yet both were destined to spend their working lives turn and turn about hauling whatever traffic presented itself.

Dolgoch was based on one of three designs prepared by Whitehaven-based Fletcher Jennings and a standard gauge one at that. It is curious that the Talyllyn Railway had two engines of different design from the same manufacturer, but that is how things turned out and, by a quirk of human nature, it was always *Talyllyn* which was the preferred choice of the enginemen on the railway. This simply resulted in her being worn out first so that *Dolgoch* came into the limelight in the twilight and early preservation years of the railway.

Dolgoch was made to Fletcher's Patent No. 321 of 1864. The invention "consist of working the valve gearing.. from an axle of the engine other than the driving axle... It is also proposed... to place the driving axle of the engine under the firebox." The object was to achieve a longer and more balanced wheelbase so that the engine could run safely at higher speeds than in usual industrial service, not that the need for that was exactly paramount on the Talyllyn Railway.

Traffic on the Talyllyn Railway made few real demands on its locomotives, which almost certainly explains why they survived so long with so little skilled attention. The only major work known to have been carried out on *Dolgoch* in her 85 years in traffic before preservation consisted of boiler repairs at the Portmadoc Britannia Foundry in 1938 and at the Shrewsbury Atlas Foundry in 1945. During this whole period, the original boiler barrel and inner firebox remained intact, as did the cylinder castings, wheels and motion.

Author and historian, James Boyd, takes up the tale and sets the scene well as regards *Dolgoch*:

"It was impossible to engage either full forward or full reverse gear due to wear in the motion, although the gear had to be used to stop the train, there being only only brake block left. The driver, who also had to repair the track, did not like using *Dolgoch* as it played havoc with his handywork. *Dolgoch* ran at about 10 mph making an appalling clatter, with one coach and three wagons loaded with sacks of flour, coal and track repairing tools, all of which pitched alarmingly in all directions.

"By Rhydyronen, pressure had fallen to 20lbs and all the company's servants huddled onto the footplate. There were no passengers, so we stopped to 'blow up'. Shortly, cows and pigs on the line impeded progress, but with every delay - though the young lad who was fireman was sent ahead to drive off the animals - the engine was able to recover breath.

"Not the stuff out of which steam locomotive nostalgia is born, but an experience repeated many times since but never with the same joy..."

By the 1950s, *Dolgoch* enjoyed longevity perhaps because her boiler was made of Low Moor iron, fitted with brass tubes and fitted with a copper firebox and the local water supply was very soft. Low Moor iron was highly resistant to corrosion and the water did not scale. Although, by modern standards, her boiler was crude and simple, the materials used were of high quality and this probably saved the day.

Tom Rolt summarised her contribution to the pioneering preservation days: "Throughout the first season of working under the Society's auspices, the responsibility of maintaining the train service fell upon No. 2 alone. Had she failed us, then our enterprise would almost certainly have come to an untimely end, and that she did not do so, though over 80 years old, is a tribute to her builders."

After the 1953 season had finished, attention turned to looking at what would be involved to repair Dolgoch. The chassis was found to be in

reasonable condition, but clearly a new boiler was needed which was built by Hunset of Leeds and delivered in 1958. The remainder of the engine was rebuilt by Griffin Brothers at Brierley Hill in the Midlands and the completed engine was returned to Towyn on 15th June, 1963. She returned to service straight away and completed 2,114 miles in her first season, followed by some considerable fiddling around to rectify faults which appeared following the rebuilding but, to all intents and purposes, the 'Old Lady' was back on her railway giving pretty good service.

She hauled the Prince and Princess of Wales on a Royal visit and has nearly always been the engine of choice for special anniversary celebrations, featuring in the centenary of the railway in 1965 and various anniversaries of the preservation era, including hauling the inaugural passenger train on the Nant Gwernol mineral extension.

Eventually, the Talyllyn Railway broke the mould of painting all their engines in mid green and branched out with Reverend Audrey 'Skarloey Railway' red. So far, she has escaped becoming 'Rheanas' but was repainted in the old company's lighter green livery for some time and now, with yet another new boiler, has been turned out in Victorian red ornately lined out as she was originally built. Of course, there is much discussion as to whether any Talyllyn engine was ever painted red... but there is one picture of her at Abergynolwyn when briefly named Pretoria clearly showing her wearing her current lining style. Until recently, it was considered that her livery then was black, but maybe it was indeed red. It is difficult to tell engine colours from old black & white pictures, especially as the photographic emulsions at those times wasn't so developed. Why is it that people get so interested about the colours an engine wears? Her current red livery suits her well and, of course, goes with the carriages. Long may the 'Old Lady' enjoy many more meanders up the beautiful Fathew Valley, hopefully with more and more passengers.

Dolgoch was repainted at the time of the Boer War and patriotically renamed *Pretoria* for a brief period. This shot shows her posed at Abergynolwyn station, possibly in the red livery she now carries, but certainly wearing the same ornate lining as she does now. For some time it was thought that *Dolgoch* was painted black during her 'Pretoria phase' but no-one can be certain as there are no longer any eye witnesses. It is perfectly possible for the engine to have then been in red livery as the photographic processes of the time often made this look black.

Pentewan

You will have heard of the Eden Project and you may well have heard of Heligan, the country house nearby where extraordinary foreign garden landscapes were created. You may well not have heard of the Pentewan Railway, just a mile or so nearby to Heligan in South Cornwall. Its historian M. J. T. Lewis aptly summaries: "The Pentewan Railway was little known in its lifetime, and little known after its death, but it well deserves wider recognition... the unusual stud of locomotives it possessed is alone sufficient to arouse the interest of the enthusiast". This then is the tale of the first of such engines, named after the railway which, in turn, was named after the sea port it served. The railway served to take china clay from St. Austell down to the port at Pentewan and was a simple mineral line of no national significance at all. In fact, its real claim to any fame (if there is even any of that) is due entirely to its bizarre locomotive policy and, in particular, one extraordinary locomotive.

> **The Pentewan Railway was little known in its lifetime, and little known after its death.**

Pentewan was manufactured by Manning Wardle of Leeds in 1873 to a most unusual design created by a Mr Fell.

John Barraclough Fell was the inventor and proponent of his own railway system called after him. It was a system designed for narrow gauge railways with a centre rail system for extra adherence on steep gradients. He particularly proposed its use when the track was mounted on a continuous low wooden viaduct and the stock fitted with horizontal guide wheels bearing against the edges of the viaduct. The alleged benefit of this apparently bizarre scheme was to save earthworks in undulating country as the wooden viaduct could simply be made to fit the contours of the land. Fell took out a patent and persuaded the War Office to trial the system at Aldershot. A railway was even constructed using his Fell system of centre rails to run over the Swiss alps. Another was used to carry trains over mountainous country in New Zealand.

The *Engineering* magazine had this to say about the patented invention; "Whether it is worthwhile doing

...the extraordinary brainchild of John Barraclough Fell

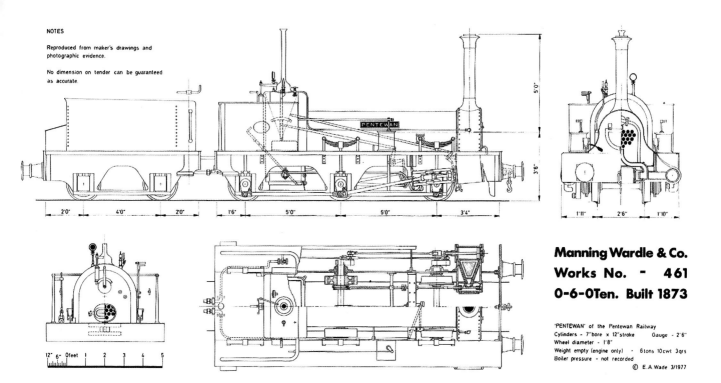

NOTES

Reproduced from maker's drawings and photographic evidence.

No dimension on tender can be guaranteed as accurate.

PENTEWAN

Manning Wardle & Co.
Works No. - 461
0-6-0Ten. Built 1873

'PENTEWAN' of the Pentewan Railway
Cylinders - 7"bore x 12"stroke   Gauge - 2'6"
Wheel diameter - 1'8"
Weight empty (engine only) - 6tons 10cwt 3qrs
Boiler pressure - not recorded

© E.A.Wade 3/1977

so much to gain so little is a point regarding which we and Mr. Fell hold very different opinions. As a means of necessitating the construction of an expensive and ridiculous form of permanent way and a type of locomotive possessing no practical advantages, Mr. Fell's plan is admirable."

The Pentewan Railway was constructed in an orthodox way but *Pentewan* was far from an orthodox 2'6" narrow gauge steam engine.

She was a six wheeled tender engine; a tender engine on the British narrow gauge is itself very unusual with only the Festiniog and Padarn railways having such locomotives at that time. The engine was made with a very low centre of gravity (such as would befit a railway built on a wooden viaduct) and her extremely tall chimney was half her overall height. Unusually, there were no fittings on her long thin boiler which aided a rather sleek appearance, enhanced by outside frames on both the engine and tender; all in all a rather attractive locomotive but most probably not a user friendly one

None of these attributes appeared to enhance the locomotive's performance. Even more extraordinarily when she wore out after only 12 years' service in 1886, the railway promptly ordered a similar replacement called *Trewithen* but pared on the cost by having her work with *Pentewan*'s tender. *Trewithen* only lasted 15 years before she too wore out, maybe the design was

flawed after all, or maybe (and possibly more likely) the maintenance was not as good as it should have been; there were rumours around the railway of some boiler explosion, but we will never know now for sure. Most probably the issue was with the long boiler and with keeping the water level within it at a satisfactory level when bouncing over uncertain track and points.

Fell was the engineer for the railway. Maybe he used his influence with the board of directors to have them order an engine derived from his patent narrow gauge system, whether out of vanity or because he hoped that a talked-of extension to Mevagissey might use his system or for some other reason we will never know. Probably the directors had no particular experience of steam locomotives and were only too happy to accept a recommendation from their engineer. Nevertheless, the design was extraordinary and, when compared with the more usual Manning Wardle engine, an 0-6-2T called *Canopus* which replaced both the two early engines, the choice looked even more peculiar. *Canopus* was sturdily built and went on to give the railway many years satisfactory service until the line was closed.

> **Whether it is worthwhile doing so much to gain so little is a point regarding which we and Mr Fell hold very different opinions.**

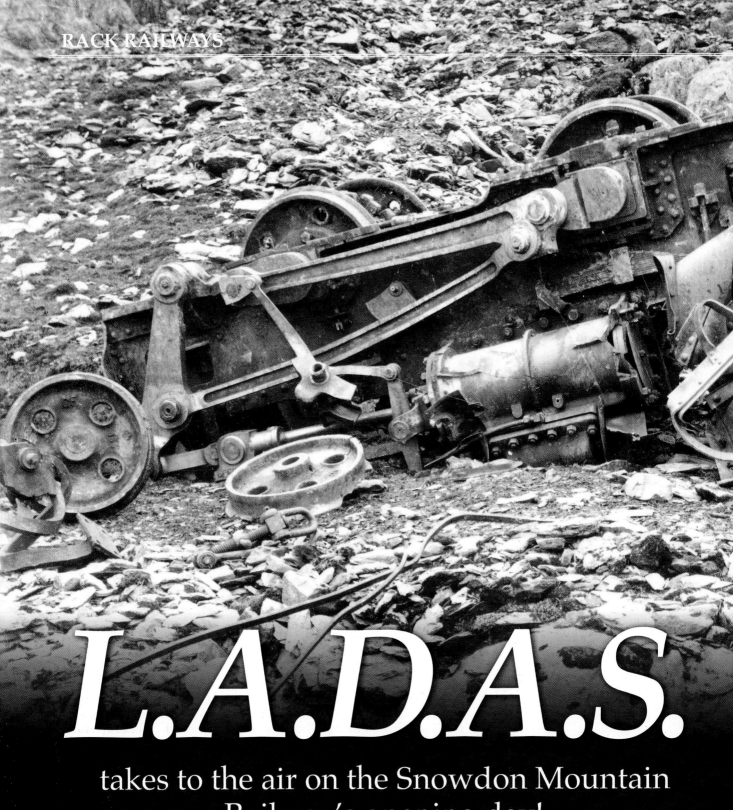

L.A.D.A.S.

takes to the air on the Snowdon Mountain Railway's opening day!

The wrecked remains of *L.A.D.A.S.* lying on the mountain side after she flew through the air. Do you have any of the pieces at home? Photo: Caernarfon Archives (Ref: XS 2221/18/11)

Easter Monday, 6th April, 1896 dawned bright and clear over Snowdon as the 150 passengers for the first public train up the mountain railway gathered at Llanberis station. Many more people who either could not afford the fare or wouldn't risk the journey were out in force to witness the proceedings. At 10.50 am engine No. 2 *Enid*, set off from the station propelling her single coach up the mountain. As every seat had been filled, it was decided to run a second train with No. 1 *L.A.D.A.S.*, using the two coaches which had previously been up the mountain with the construction workers to allow

them to celebrate ahead of time. *Enid* had been named after the daughter of the owner of both the mountain and the nearby Dinorwic Quarry, Assheton Smith. *L.A.D.A.S.* was rather incongruously named using the initials of his wife Laura Alice Duff Assheton Smith. It was to be an inauspicious day for *L.A.D.A.S.* and the only public train she would ever haul.

The journey to the summit was uneventful. But, shortly after starting the descent, the guard found that speed was increasing too much and immediately applied the brakes bringing the train to a complete stand. The driver was instructed to proceed with more caution but, shortly before reaching Clogwyn,

the first station down from the summit, disaster struck. The train gave a violent lurch, speed increased again but this time more rapidly and several of the passengers began to panic. The guard shouted to them to keep their seats but this was too late for two of the passengers who had already jumped, as they had seen the engine crew do the same. As is usual on rack & pinion railways the carriages were not coupled to the engine and so were quickly brought to a safe stop. However of L.A.D.A.S. there was nothing to be seen...

The appearance of the engine crew climbing back up the mountain revealed what had happened.

L.A.D.A.S. had mounted the rack in the cutting (later discovered to be due to settlement of the track following construction) and had quickly gathered speed running headlong down the mountain. The engine crew had jumped off as they realised that No. 1 was, by now, completely uncontrollable, since all the brakes only worked if the engine was engaged on the rack. They were both uninjured, but L.A.D.A.S. was not so lucky. She gained momentum, hit a corner in the track, left the rails and leapt over the side of the mountain, flying over the bridle path to the astonishment of walkers climbing steadily up the mountain. After all it is not every day that a steam engine flies over peoples' heads. L.A.D.A.S. was later found at the bottom of a 300ft precipice below the railway: boiler amazingly intact but the rest of the engine scattered in pieces all down the mountain. No. 1 had struck the rocks at the foot of the cliff which had sheared the boiler from the frames and which, quite remarkably, had landed with virtually no damage and was later recovered to spend the rest of its working days as a stationary boiler in the quarry. The remainder of the engine which was not recoverable was left to its fate and souvenir hunters; maybe one day the nameplates will surface from some mountain walker's family collection.

Coloured McCorquedale postcard produced as part of the London & North Western Railway collection showing the SMR as it was intended to operate with a two coach train. It is almost certain that this picture, taken on the second main viaduct out of Llanberis, was posed before the line was open.

As if this was not enough disaster for one day, No. 2 *Enid* had set off from the summit without signalling clearance. Instructions had been to await a signal that the first down train had cleared Clogwyn but, unfortunately, when *L.A.D.A.S.* left the rails, she smashed into a telegraph pole so rendering the signalling system inoperable, but causing a bell to be rung at the summit which, erroneously but understandably, gave the impression that the line to

> ... *She gained momentum... left the rails... and leapt over the side of the mountain, flying over the bridle path to the astonishment of walkers climbing up the mountain.*

Clogwyn was then clear, so No. 2 started the descent at a dead slow speed. By now clouds had descended so visibility was impaired. No. 2's driver felt his engine lurch in the cutting at the same place as *L.A.D.A.S.* had done but, fortunately, No. 2 regained the rack and so continued downhill. But visibility was now only a matter of feet and so the second train bore down on the first, narrowly missing the passengers who had by now detrained. Their frantic hand waving for No. 2 to stop went un-noticed and *Enid* ploughed into the back of the two empty coaches of the first train which were standing on the rails following the first disaster. The impact sent both coaches hurtling down the steep slope towards Clogwyn. Fortunately, the pointsman there managed to change the points to direct the uncontrollable coaches into the loop where they derailed, with one leaning over on its side. This scene was immortalized in a picture postcard taken the following day and which must have done wonders for encouraging future passengers, although no doubt sales of the card were high as it was printed in great numbers and is often found in antique postcard fair sales even today.

Passenger made their way dow the mountain and *Enid* and the remaining carriages were left where they stood. No further trains were run that day and all public services were suspended until further

Snowdon Train

Enid comes to rest after colliding with the carriages of the second train and is propped up by wooden poles to prevent further catastrophe.
Photo: Caernarfon Archives (Ref XS 2221/18/9)

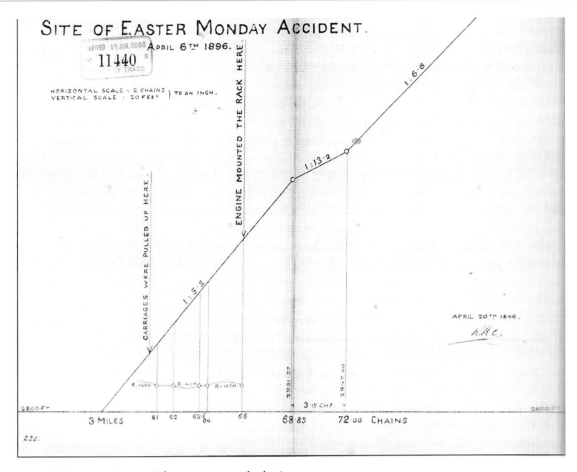

SITE OF EASTER MONDAY ACCIDENT.

APRIL 6TH 1896.

RECEIVED 15 JUN 1896.
11440

HORIZONTAL SCALE : 2 CHAINS } TO AN INCH.
VERTICAL SCALE : 20 FEET }

ENGINE MOUNTED THE RACK HERE.

CARRIAGES WERE PULLED UP HERE.

1:13·2

1:5·5

1:6·6

APRIL 20TH 1896.

2800 FT

3 MILES 61 62 63·5/64 66 68·85 72·00 CHAINS

235.

notice. Unfortunately, one of the passengers who had jumped, but fell back under the train as he did so, first lost his leg through amputation and then died in hospital in the early hours of the following day.

The future of the Snowdon Mountain Railway was in the balance. At the subsequent enquiry, it was agreed that the track in the offending place had subsided due to the shaley nature of the rock it was laid on and the effect of recent snow and ice when it thawed and drained away. The weight of the first two trains on the opening day were the final straw, resulting in *L.A.D.A.S.*'s rack pinions becoming disengaged as she passed over the offending rails, throwing the engine completely out of control. The Board of Trade recommended adding further safety devices which was done and then the unenviable task began of rebuilding the railway's reputation and recommencing services.

Somewhat naturally, questions were asked about the safety of mountain rack railway lines and the Swiss Abt rack system used. Faced with a possible slight to its reputation, the Abt company wrote to *The Engineer* magazine with its views. Interestingly, it had made an inspection of the Snowdon Mountain Railway itself prior to opening and was not satisfied as to the standard of construction work. There was one rather telling paragraph in its report: "When all the facts are considered, it must not be overlooked that the accident happened to the first regular train at the opening of the railway; that this first train was composed of two carriages with full load, which is the specified maximum; that the line was entirely new and still in an unfinished and unsettled condition; that the time of the year was rather early and the frost hardly yet out of the ground, that the drivers, able as they may be, could not be supposed to have already acquired sufficient experience at once with a full load".

Postscript

The last word on the incidents of the opening day must fall to a Mr McFarlane of Glasgow. He had the misfortune to be climbing up Snowdon for the first time around the craggy recesses of the Cwmglas gully when the accident took place. He recalls that the shock of meeting a live steam engine rapidly flying overhead out of the mist only yards away from him led to his immediate non-stop departure for Conwy as fast as he could go... or so the story goes...!

Mountain Railway from Snowdon

Swiss Moun

Below: Two steam trains descend the Brienz Rothorn mountain, the first train has a single coach, being the capacity of the original series of locomotives; the second train has two, being within the capacity of the larger second series 1936 batch of engines.

Until the nineteenth century, it was not possible to travel easily and most people had precious little leisure time. Railways changed all that as far as land transport was concerned and soon holidaying was able to become more adventurous. Of course, some people had been mountaineering for years, but, generally, it was the advent of the railways and their branch lines opening up previously remote country which made mountaineering a much more accessible hobby

A 1914 booklet entitled *Holidays in North Wales* comments on developments in the pastime: "North Wales is essentially a mountainous country and offers every inducement to the mountain climber, some of the ascents being gentle and gradual, but others of supreme difficulty and requiring all the nerve and resource of a member of the Alpine Club". It suggests a trip to the summit of Snowdon by mountain railway and describes it as "a line built on the system in use on the Alpine and similar railways and is the only one of its kind in the British Isles. It is worked on the principle of a number of cog wheels engaging in a continuous rack or perforated plateway laid between the rails, and may be pronounced as absolutely safe in working, the material throughout having been submitted to careful tests far beyond any possible strain it may be called upon to bear."

"... a line built on the system in use on Alpine railways and is the only one of its kind in the British Isles ..."

tain Engines

The Snowdon Mountain Railway was built following the Swiss design and was, in fact, a railway system imported from Switzerland which makes it doubly unique in the British Isles. At that time Britain had no knowledge of constructing rack railways or locomotives. However, in narrow gauge terms, the Swiss were only a few years ahead as the Brienz Rothorn mountain railway, of the same two foot seven and a half inch (800 millimetre) gauge had only opened in 1892, whereas the first sod on the SMR was cut just two years later on 5th December, 1894, with the railway initially opening to the public at Easter in 1896.

SUMMIT OF CADER IDRIS.

Actually, the first two rack railways in the world were both standard gauge and, although a Swiss can claim to be the inventor, it was down to an American, Sylvestor Marsh, to construct the very first mountain rack railway in the world on Mount Washington in New Hampshire. He was an American entrepreneur who had been forced to spend the night on the mountain in bad weather at the mercy of the elements. He retired from his business and determined to build a railway up the three miles on the mountain to the summit with the idea of using a 'rack' cogwheel to climb the severe gradients. Work commenced as early as 1867.

This spurred Niklaus Riggenbach to do something. In 1863 Riggenbach, a Swiss engineer, took out a patent for a method of operating trains up steep gradients; his idea was also to carry passengers up to the famous mountain viewpoints in his country. His plan was similar, to anchor between the running rails a steel ladder for his locomotives which would be equipped with vertical toothed wheels driven by steam cylinders and engaging with the rack (and so coining the 'rack and pinion' name). But, although he registered a patent, he did no more until he heard that Sylvester had actually built a similar type of railway in the USA. Riggenback hurried over to

Above: **Summit of Cader Idris: a commercial postcard showing the new Victorian pastime of mountain climbing.**

Snowdon Mountain Railway steam engines

1. *L.A.D.A.S*	built 1895 SLM Works	No. 923 (destroyed 1896)
2. *Enid*	built 1895 SLM Works	No. 924
3. *Wyddfa*	built 1896 SLM Works	No. 925
4. *Snowdon*	built 1896 SLM Works	No. 988
5. *Moel Siabod*	built 1896 SLM Works	No. 989
6. *Padarn*	built 1922 SLM Works	No. 2838 (originally *Sir Harmood*)
7. *Aylwin*	built 1923 SLM Works	No. 2869
8. *Eryri*	built 1923 SLM Works	No. 2870

Above: **SLM advert for its rack locomotives and publicity material for the Brienz Rothorn Bahn and Snowdon Mountain Railway.**

Above right: **The Rigi Bahn, the first European rack mountain railway setting the scene for enormous tourist traffic to the top of Swiss, European and Welsh mountains by means of rack and pinion systems.**

New Hampshire to see this pioneer railway and then formed a company without any further delay, obtained a concession from the Canton of Lucerne and built the Rigi Railway from Vitznau on the lake, but again of standard gauge. The Pilatus mountain railway, on the other side of the lake, used the narrow gauge and was constructed to a much steeper gradient requiring additional wheels to ensure a safe grip.

The Swiss mountain line which is perhaps the most similar to the Snowdon Mountain Railway, simply because it is of the same gauge, is the Brienz Rothorn line which runs from Brienz on the edge of the lake of the same name up to the summit of the Brienzer Rothorn mountain in the Bernese Oberland. It still uses some of its 1892 steam engines for heritage journeys but has since acquired two more modern designs, one from 1936 and the other, probably being the most modern type of steam engine in the world, a series built at SLM Winterthur in 1992. These are oil fired,

one man operated and are plugged into a thermostat at night to aid steam raising in the morning. The Brienz Rothorn Railway had previously determined to move to diesel haulage but changed its mind when this modern rack engine type was designed and now has four examples which run most trains. Whilst they are indeed steam, their exhaust beat is most disappointing

Above left: **The Brienz Rothorn Railway climbs high above Lake Brienz into highly dramatic mountain scenery.**

Above right: **Wengernalp, the penultimate station before Kleine Scheidegg, the junction terminus between the Wengernalp Bahn and the Jungfrau Bahn. A commercial postcard from 1906 showing Edwardian tourists dressed in their finery. This line is now fully electrified and carries over 700,000 tourists each year.**

Left: **Keeping the tracks open for the ski-ing season: a snowplough train on the French Chemin de Fer de Glion-Naye.**

The Brienz Rothorn Bahn's first steam rack locomotive, No. I on shed at Brienz.

BRB No. 6, 1936 second series locomotive on shed at Brienz.

and, in motion, they sound rather like a superior lawn mower; but at least they are still steam and as such remain very popular with the public. The line is really well worth a ride as its formation is most dramatic. After climbing above the town of Brienz, through mountain pastures, the line runs through a series of tunnels cut in the cliff face with openings to see down on the lake below; the train of passengers never fail to exclaim plenty of "oos" and "ahs" when the train runs through these tunnels as the combination of the engine noise and steam with the stupendous views is superb. Not satisfied with this, once water has been taken at Planalp in the high mountain pastures, the line climbs round three sides of a serrated ridge and then plunges into one last horseshoe tunnel before bursting out to the top terminus just before the summit. Would that the Snowdon Mountain Railway was as equally dramatic, but it is not; it simply and adequately climbs a ridge all the way from Llanberis to the summit.

In addition to the track gauge and the similar style of locomotives, both the Brienz Rothorn and the Snowdon Mountain Railway share a third similarity: they both use the Abt rack system. Roman Abt had been appointed by Riggenbach as his chief construction engineer and, during this time, Abt developed his own rack system which was a considerable advance on Riggenbach's and he patented it in 1882. The essential difference between the two systems was the type of rack assembly used: Riggenbach used a ladder system laid between the running rails, whereas Abt designed a single rack bar, with vertically facing teeth machined out of it, also laid in the centre of the running rails. This had two advantages: the rack 'teeth' could not possibly work loose as they were an integral part of the bar. Secondly, as the rack and also the pinion on the locomotive were both machined, a much more accurate 'fit' could be achieved. Furthermore, the Abt system could be made even safer by laying two rack bars side by side and, by 'staggering' the rack teeth and, by using double pinions on the locomotive, a

continuous grip was ensured between the locomotive and the track. However, as we have seen in the essay about *L.A.D.A.S.*, even such a 'fool proof' system was not perfect if not carefully laid and tested in the first place...

The SMR steam engines are pure Swiss and the only examples of their type now running anywhere in the world outside Switzerland. Sadly, not all the locomotives are now in running order, although the railway has recently announced a plan to offer a steam heritage service for the first time. It would be entirely appropriate for one of the Swiss-built Snowdon Mountain Railway engines to be preserved on display in the National Railway Museum as they are a significant item of railway engineering totally absent from the display.

BRB SLM's third series 1992 design one man-operated steam rack locomotive takes water at Planalp.

Above: **SMR wheelset in Llanberis workshop showing the Abt system engine pinion.**

Right: **System Abt No. 4 on the BRB.**

Below right: **SLM Winterthur 1936 works plate of BRB second series locomotive.**

Below: **SMR's first series locomotive No. 4 Snowdon on shed at Llanberis.**

SMRs second series locomotive No. 6 *Padarn.*

The steam rack engine is a six-wheeled locomotive developed by the Swiss Locomotive and Machine Works. When one looks at the engine from the track side, it appears to be an 0-4-2T and is commonly mistaken as such. The reason it is not so, is because only the pinions and not the carrying wheels are coupled, so each track interfacing wheel rotates separately. The second misconception about steam rack locomotives is that they work even harder than ordinary railway locomotives, simply because of the steep grades they work up. In fact, the various demands on the locomotive are far more uniform than for an 'ordinary' engine. The locomotive is not subject to widely varying loads or speeds; it is designed to suit its particular work which is always uniform. Of course, the work is hard but the locomotive is robust and straightforward and needs no thrashing. It is intended to work primarily at a maximum cut off of 80% and never less than 60%. If speeds were not strictly limited to between 4 and 5 mph, the strain on the engine and its boiler would be an entirely different matter. At 5 mph, an automatic steam governor comes into play, cutting off steam and applying the steam brake. This steady demand for steam ensures a surprisingly long life for the whole machine and, with the exception of their boilers, the original parts of the Snowdon Mountain engines have mainly survived.

The engines originally cost £1,400 each and were transported from Winterthur, some 13 miles from Zurich, all the way to Llanberis. An eye witness of their arrival recorded: "the engines arrived at Llanberis LNWR on flat wagons and they were the lowered onto temporary tracks; three rail lengths laid end to end and then drawn forward by traction engines. Horses then pulled the two rearward rail lengths to the front in readiness for a fresh advance. The coaches were just horse-hauled along the high-road on their own wheels, apparently without damage to the macadamised surface. Naturally, Llanberis turned out to view these exotic arrivals, whose only claims to kinship were the familiar local names borne on the brass nameplates of the locomotives."

Again, a similar locomotive policy has been followed by both the Snowdon Mountain Railway and the Swiss Brienz Rothorn line. An original batch of steam engines was supplied for the opening of the railway, then in the 1920s (for the SMR) and the 1930s (for the BRB) more modern steam engines were supplied. Both lines turned to diesel traction in more modern times, but so far only the BRB has returned to steam to haul nearly all its trains with the modern SLM design.

The new generation of oil-fired steam rack locomotives built by SLM in the 1990s were essentially a development of the BRB 1930s locomotives which themselves had an updated geared design. Four are now in service on the BRB and further examples work on the two rack lines in Austria.

SLM 1992 works plate.

Little Railways
for Pleasure
...BUT WITH COMMERCIAL ASPIRATIONS

Ella is seen here when new at Tennis Ground station in 1881.

Right: *Southern Maid* on shed at Hythe. At a quick glance this hardly seems any different to the real thing.

Arthur Percival Heywood lived in the golden age of railways, was trained as an engineer and was wealthy enough to indulge in his hobby to the full. He had the idea that a 15 inch gauge railway was the minimum gauge which could replace the horse and cart to do a job of work. The result was his garden railway at Duffield Bank in Derbyshire, which he used to demonstrate his idea, and also as a fabulous garden railway for his family.

His view was that such a railway would be a most useful economic form of transport for country estates, farms and other institutions. He convinced the Duke of Westminster to build such a line at his Eaton Hall residence in Cheshire, but that was all and the idea otherwise died with him, although 15 inch gauge railways became all the rage as pleasure railways and several still survive as such today.

In the summer of 1874, Arthur Heywood was invited to Aldershot to attend the trials of John Barraclough Fell's proposed military railway system (whom we encountered in the essay on *Pentewan*). The army were looking for a suitable narrow gauge railway system for issue to the Royal Engineers and kept ready for use with trained men which could be laid down from a standard gauge railhead to the trenches. Fell's proposal

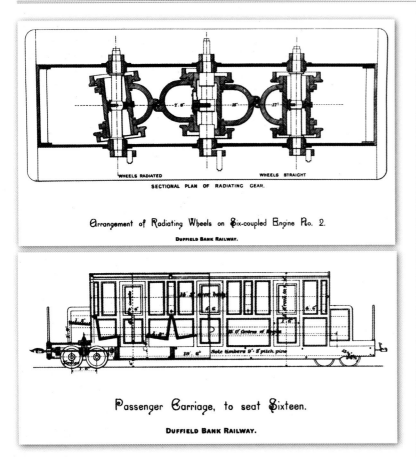

SECTIONAL PLAN OF RADIATING GEAR.

WHEELS RADIATED   WHEELS STRAIGHT

Arrangement of Radiating Wheels on Six-coupled Engine No. 2.

DUFFIELD BANK RAILWAY.

Passenger Carriage, to seat Sixteen.

DUFFIELD BANK RAILWAY.

Top: **Sectional plan of Heywood locomotive radiating wheels on a six coupled engine.**

Above: **Drawing of passenger carriage to seat 16 people.**

Early memories...

"As a child I was often taken to the Fairbourne Railway where I always hoped that *Count Louis* would be working rather than *Dingo* the petrol engine. I was often disappointed. Maybe because *Count Louis* seemed to run so infrequently on my visits, I wanted to see the engine even more. Then, one day, seeing him all forlorn under a tarpaulin, it occurred to me that I could put him back into working order. Brett Rogers and I decided to do just that but on the pre-condition that our children, Stuart and Charlotte, were the future owners. *Count Louis* thus lives on." MW

A specially posed view of *Ella* and a train on a hairpin bend on the Duffield Bank Railway; the train is too long and heavy for the engine to have hauled in reality, but makes an impressive picture!

Zbrowski held wild parties flowing with champagne, tied pretty damsels to the railway track, had his engine driven towards them but rescued them in the nick of time!

was an eighteen inch gauge elevated line mounted on trestles which could be constructed to any height to save earthworks. The army did not like this but did adopt both eighteen inch and two foot railways for warfare use; but not Heywood's 15 inch 'minimum gauge', although Heywood was convinced he could produce something better.

He developed his garden railway at Duffield Bank as an experiment and the Royal Agricultural Show held in Derby near his home in 1881 proved to be the ideal opportunity to show it off. Heywood issued invitations to visit his railway and wrote a pamphlet about its virtues.

His 'little engines' proved to be works of engineering art, built with best materials and were constructed with several innovative features, including a radial gear to permit them to go round very tight radii curves. The innovation was described like this: "The wheels were not fixed directly to the axles but to sleeves through which the axles passed. In the case of the middle

axle, the sleeve was splined so that motion could be communicated to the wheels, while at the same time the wheels could move up to one inch either way laterally. Thus, on a curve, the wheels were drawn by the arc of the rails to one side by an amount equal to the versed sign of the arc."

After trialling a few prototypes, Heywood commissioned a six coupled engine named *Ella* in time to take part in the Royal Agricultural Society meeting's visit. One fine summer's day' *Ella* left the Duffield bank workshop resplendent in her dark green livery lined out in red and gold and the visitors showed much interest in her. To find out the maximum load she would haul, she was tried out and found to be able to haul a load of four tons - some 14 cwts more than her own weight - up a quarter of a mile run of 1 in 10.

Heywood also built a remarkable collection of carriages to accompany his magnificent little engines, in order to further his garden railway hobby and

Heywood *Muriel* in use at the Ratty as a stationary boiler in May 1927.
Photo: A.W.Croughton

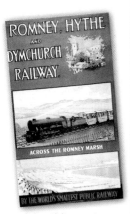

Advertising poster for the RH&D proclaiming the line to be the World's smallest public railway; the picture shows the excellence of the locomotive engineering but the comparative penny pinching of the rolling stock.

> **One day, Howey steamed up a 'Royal Scot' model in his living room whilst his wife was away just to see what happened. Of course, he had to redecorate the whole room.**

provide entertainment for his family and their guests. These included a dining car and, amazingly, a sleeping car, both suitably equipped and both used for their intended purpose. He would lay on a 'night trip' for friends, beginning with dinner in the dining car, after which the passengers bedded down in the sleeping car and were taken round the track all through the night with intervals for the engine to take on coal and water!

Sadly, nothing much survives of Heywood's railways, although a section of the Eaton Hall Railway has been rebuilt with a replica engine called *Katie* running with some original rolling stock. All the Heywood equipment was dispersed at auction on his death, but most went on to perform useful roles on other miniature railways run for pleasure, so we will look at three of perhaps the key such lines next.

Cab view of *Ursula* at Muncaster Mill on the Ratty; the driver has to perch on the rear handrail when driving and stand behind the engine when firing the marine-type firebox.

In 1904, model engineer W.J. Bassett Lowke and Henry Greenly formed a company called Miniature Railways of Great Britain Limited to build and operate miniature railways for entertainment at seaside resorts using scale model steam engines designed by Greenly and called 'Little Giants'. They too chose 15 inches as their standard gauge, doubtless influenced by Heywood. The first of their engines was even tested at Eaton Hall. Whilst many of their seaside lines ebbed and flowed with the tourism trade (and some were hurriedly dismantled to prevent bailiffs seizing them when finances ran out!), some have survived in developed form to continue to give pleasure to many; perhaps the most famous three are the Romney Hythe & Dymchurch Railway in Kent, the Ravenglass Eskdale Railway in the English Lake District (known as the 'Ratty')and (although now reguaged to twelve and a quarter inches), the Fairbourne Railway in Wales.

Bassett Lowke, Greenly and associates formed another company to take over the ailing three foot narrow gauge railway in the Lake District running up from the sea at Ravenglass to Boot under England's highest mountain, Scafell. They converted it to their own standard gauge of 15 inches and arranged for Bassett Lowke's model engineering company to equip it with miniature steam engines, but also purchased some of the Heywood engines (*Katie* and *Muriel*) and some of the coaches. *Katie* was not up to the task of hauling tourists for seven miles and so was sold on, eventually ending up at the Fairbourne Railway having got a reputation as a bad steamer, probably as a result of the firing techniques required to keep her launch-type boiler under full pressure. *Muriel*, however, still survives, although much rebuilt and now renamed *River Irt*, but fundamentally the chassis, motion and wheelsets are still to the original design. The Greenly-designed Bassett Lowke miniature quarter scale engines were not up to the task either and the position was not helped by some head on collisions reducing the availability of the locomotive fleet! However, Greenly was an excellent miniature

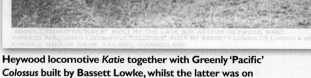

Heywood locomotive *Katie* together with Greenly 'Pacific' *Colossus* built by Bassett Lowke, whilst the latter was on trial on the Duke of Westminster's Eaton Hall railway.

Above: **Replica Heywood six coupled side tank** *Ursula,* **built by James Waterfield, seen on the turntable at Ravenglass.**

Count Louis, **after spending a lifetime's service on the Fairbourne Miniature Railway, double-heads fellow Bassett Lowke Class 30** *Synolda* **on the Ravenglass & Eskdale Railway on a private charter for the Heywood Society of miniature railway afficionados. The 'Ratty' used to run the third Class 30** *Sans Pareil* **in its early 15" gauge days and so has seen all three members of the class operate over its line.**

'Little Giant' Class 10 *Prince Edward of Wales* on the Rhyl Pleasure Park railway circulating round the marine lake.

Colossus the first 15in gauge 'Atlantic' type 4-6-2 made for Captain J.E.P. Howey and only the second 'Atlantic' type in the country, after the GWR's *Great Bear*.

'Little Giant' Class 20 *Prince Edward of Wales* at Barmouth Ferry on the Fairbourne Railway amongst the sand which played havoc with the valve gear and motion on the model engines.

'Little Giant' Class 30 *Sans Pareil* and former Heywood coaches on the Ratty.

Right inset: **Replica Heywood dining car all laid up ready for dinner.**

railway engineer and soon designed a suitable steam engine from scratch which has proved to be a mainstay for the line ever since: *River Esk*, a 2-8-2 and made to one third scale. This set the tone for all the R&ER's subsequent steam motive power and several engines have subsequently been built following its image, notably *River Mite* and also, in the railway's own workshops (but with a bought in boiler), *Northern Rock*. This famous miniature line has experienced various financial crises over the years but now seems on a stable footing supported by a preservation society but still privately owned by Lord Wakefield's family.

The Fairbourne Railway, opposite to the seaside town of Barmouth was also developed into a miniature railway by the Bassett Lowke team. Originally, it was built as a horse tramway by McDougall of flour fame, but the miniature railwayists saw an opportunity to develop it at the same time as holiday makers were starting to flock to the seaside in Wales for summer holidays. Barmouth had no sandy beaches, but the Fairbourne peninsula opposite did. So, combining with the thrifty Barmouth ferrymen, the 15 inch line did quite well during the holiday boom and had one of the 'Little Giant' type engines assigned to it named *Prince Edward of Wales*.

This was upgraded to a Class 30 'Little Giant' type; the third and largest variant of which only three were built. *Count Louis* came to the line to stay to the end of its 15 inch gauge career and so be synonymous to many holidaymakers with the Fairbourne Railway image. *Count Louis* was built by Bassett Lowke for Count Louis Zbrowski, an extremely rich Polish motor racing fanatic who lived his life in the fast lane. He ordered the Class 30 to run at his house at Highams in Kent and held wild parties flowing with champagne, tied pretty damsels to the railway track, had his engine driven towards them but rescued them in the nick of time! He died as he lived, driving too fast resulting in a motor racing accident in his Bentley at Le Mans. Had he not done so, the 15 inch miniature railway world might have been very

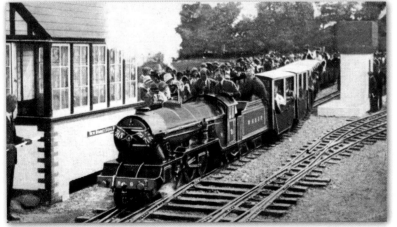

The Duke of York driving *Northern Chief* on the RH&D's opening day on 6th August, 1926 from New Romney station with Captain J.E.P. Howey also on the footplate and Nigel Gresley, the designer of the standard gauge 'real thing' sitting on the back of the tender.

different. He had teamed up with John Howey, another millionaire, to build (just for fun) a miniature railway to run fast trains on over the Kent marsh flatlands. Together they commissioned Greenley to design and Paxmans to build two magnificent one third scale models of the then current and famous LNER 'Pacifics'; no expense spared. The two men even went to see if they should buy the Ravenglass & Eskdale Railway and extend it through a long tunnel under Hard Knott Pass to Ambleside! They were both rich enough and mad enough to have done it. Even though Zbrowski did not live to fulfill his miniature railway ambitions, Howey did and, also, *Count Louis*,

as the Highams Class 30 was named after the Count's death, went on to become an icon in itself and is now preserved and still in running order by the editor, Brett Rogers and family as a true 'Gentleman's' light sporting locomotive'! The Fairbourne Railway lived on, changing hands twice to be owned by rich individuals (as befits the design and standing of railways of such a gauge): John Wilkins, manufacturer of Servis washing machines kept the line running as a 'business hobby' until he died, but then it was bought and regauged by John Ellerton so that he could use his twelve and a quarter inch gauge engines and rolling stock on it and it has now passed on to a trust

Above: **Northern Rock built in the Ratty's Ravenglass workshops and sponsored by the Building Society carrying the engine's name but still, nevertheless, appropriate to the geography of the railway; the train is approaching Eskdale Green.**

River Mite breaks a ribbon at the Ratty's Dalegarth terminus station at the end of its inaugural run from Ravenglass on 20th May, 1967; the engine was commissioned by the supporters' association specially for the railway and was the first modern eight coupled steam engine built for the preservation regime. Photo: J.A. Ingram

River Esk designed by Greenly and built by Paxman at Ravenglass still with the three foot gauge station building and Heywood rolling stock. This engine was the first miniature design specially for the Ratty and used an eight coupled chassis. Photo: A.W. Croughton

In the early days of the second world war, when invasion seemed imminent, one of the protection measures taken was to provide armoured trains to run on the coast railways, including the miniature RH&D! Eight coupled *Hercules* was armour plated for patrol in 1941; whilst the railway suffered some bomb damage, the armoured train survived unscathed.

The real thing *Flying Scotsman* meets *Southern Maid* at a Tyseley open day in Birmingham.

This picture is interesting for three reasons: (a) it depicts one of the two 'Mountain' type 4-8-2s *Hercules*, (b) he wears the 'Marshlander' headboard of the line's crack express train; and (c) the engine is sitting on Hythe turntable which was formerly used by the equally famous Lynton & Barnstaple Railway in their Pilton Yard; maybe one day they will want it back.

Howey and Zbrowski's dream: a double track main line in miniature with easy grades for very fast running by expertly crafted one third scale Gresley 'Pacifics'.

but fallen on stony times as tourists really no longer come to Fairbourne. The course of the river has changed and Barmouth now has sandy beaches of its own...

The last tale in this essay has to be about probably the most outlandish 15 inch miniature railway of all in the British Isles: the Romney, Hythe & Dymchurch Railway built, as one man's railway and to last but his lifetime. So true was this, that when Howey died, pretty much the whole railway and its equipment had to be rebuilt as it was by then life expired. Fortunately, philanthropists saw to it that it was, so we can still enjoy the line as originally built, albeit with more housing by the lineside than ever before.

Howey started off with another miniature railway engine too, just like Zbrowski, and it too was made by Bassett Lowke. But Howey had to go one better and have a 'Pacifics' design built called *John Anthony*, only the second engine of its type anywhere in the country at that time, the other example being the GWR *Great Bear*. He soon moved on though, selling the engine to the R&ER to build the RH&D simply because he could. Howey's father had lived in Australia and staked out a square mile of land which was to become the city centre of Melbourne. So Howey never had to do a day's work in his life and could do exactly what he liked. He did pretty well just that. One day, at home in Kent, he steamed up a ten and quarter gauge 'Royal Scot' steam engine in his living room whilst his wife was away just

The RH&DR 'Pacifics' have been painted all colours and all shades to distinguish them. Here we see *Hurricane* looking extremely smart in Caledonian Railway blue, with emphasis on her very large tender, designed so as to provide enough water for a complete non-stop run from Hythe, through New Romney, round the Dymchurch loop and all the way back again.

Postscript

One significant new miniature railway, built to Sir Arthur's minimum gauge is the Bure Valley Railway which re-opened a former Great Eastern Railway branch line from Wroxham to Aylesham in 1990 at a cost of £2.5million. It is actually the longest sub standard gauge railway in Norfolk and, as it is built on a standard gauge railway formation, it has some serious 1in100 hills to climb but also space on the formation for a parallel long distance footpath. It successfully carries over 130,000 passengers a year

It can claim several ties to the 'old hands' in fifteen inch gauge which are discussed in this essay. When first open, it relied on hired in locomotives from the Romney Hythe & Dymchurch Railway but, as these are large wheeled pacifics designed by Greenly and used by Howey for 'racing', something better at hill climbing was needed. So a bespoke 2-6-2 tender engine design was produced, modelled on the Indian ZB type and two are now in service

They are joined by three tank engines, one of which was formerly on the Fairbourne Railway called Tracey Jo. Its outline followed the Vale of Rheidol tank engines, although it was originally powered by diesel. Now, it is a steam engine (as it always should have been) named Wroxham Broad and spends some of its time helping out on the Ravenglass & Eskdale line. So, the Bure Valley Railway can certainly claim fame by association, but it is also a successful line in its own right in a good tourist market. Welcome aboard!

to see what happened. Of course, he had to redecorate the whole room...!

Howey selected the Kent marshlands so that he could run trains on his railway at speed on a double track miniature version of the East Coast Main Line! Not for nothing did he order the one third sized LNER 'Pacifics' and he didn't stop at two either. The railway ended up with five LNER 'Pacifics', two 4-8-2s and two Canadian style 'Pacifics' for good measure. Two of the LNER style 'Pacifics' even had three cylinders and one of these was Howey's special pet named *Hurricane*. Howey managed to run it up to a good 50 mph. That was nothing; he converted one of his Rolls Royce cars to 15 inch gauge and ran that up to 60mph!

To get the 'authorities' to allow Howey to build the RH&D, he had to agree to run a public service. To do this, he built a pretty ramshackle set of passenger coaches which certainly didn't match the excellence of his locomotives, but the holidaying public were a stoic lot before the war and put up with most things just to have a ride. Howey was often to be seen driving.

Howey was a man who did things with panache and invited the then Duke of York, later to be King George VI, to drive the line's opening train and for the famous Laurel & Hardy comedians to visit in 1947. Not all went Howey's way though and, during the second world war, the army requisitioned part of the line as a sea defence and even converted a train into an armoured

gun unit for patrolling! At least, if Heywood had known, he would have been proud that at last a 15 inch gauge train had been used by the military!

Fortunately, all these public miniature railways are still with us in some shape or form and very many others have been built, either as pleasure railways for the public or simply as private garden railways for miniature railway engineers and their families. Like Heywood's railway, they are transient though, and often disappear after the life of the promoter only to reappear later on in some other disguise or form elsewhere. So be it.

The Woosung
...an unwanted railway

However heavy the piece to be carried, its transport is only a matter of the skilful arrangement of bamboos, ropes and plenty of labour. So, *Pioneer*, weighing 26 cwt empty, was carried by 16 men a distance of four furlongs without so much as pausing to draw breath.

Richard Rapier, whose East Anglian Ransomes & Rapier business majored in the production of agricultural equipment, was always on the look out for another deal and the means to promote to new markets. In the 1870s China had no railways and Rapier had the idea of presenting the new 18 year old Emperor with a short railway. If he was seen to use it, then surely noblemen and officials would wish to follow suit and British exports would benefit. He was to be proved badly wrong.

However, Rapier was well connected within the British Isles at least and so he approached the Duke of Sutherland with the idea which was then discussed with several of the promoters for the Isle of Man Railway including Pender and Loch, the latter having previous experience of diplomatic missions to China. They did not dismiss it and indeed the idea grew and received substantial support from notables in railway engineering circles such as Tyler, Vignoles, Manning and Peacock.

The young emperor died and that might have been that. However, Rapier had already built a small engine to the 2'6" gauge speculatively. Jardine, Matheson & Co, the famous far eastern trading house, inspected it and as they had already acquired a small strip of Chinese land between Shanghai and Woosung, agreed to assist. They too were to be proved badly wrong. Buying land with a view to putting a road on it is one thing, but they assumed they could also lay a railway on it. Whilst there was no law saying that they could not, neither was there a law saying they could. With hindsight,

❝...Engine ran today. Chinese delighted❞

Railway

The first 'permanent train' on the Woosung line hauled by *Celestial Empire* with *Pioneer* on the construction train behind.

it was somewhat amazing that they ventured forth and persevered, as it was all to end in tears.

China had no railways but, to Western eyes it was logical that it should, as railways were well known to create beneficial trading opportunities by opening up hinterlands. Despite the knowledge and connection that there must have been about China, all the promoters had overlooked one critical fact. The Empire of China is like no other. Descended from a remote antiquity, her rulers have always held the doctrine that China is the Middle Kingdom, the fountain of all knowledge and advancement and that any suggestions coming from the west must, in the nature of things, be retrogressive.

Even the great and powerful trading company of Jardine Matheson had been disappointed in their efforts to introduce railways into China. Roads were,

> **A general cry of "Laij tze, laij tze... it is coming... it is coming" heralds each return journey.**

however, another matter and the custom had grown that, in all the European settlements in China, their construction had to be undertaken by Europeans. The company were now of the opinion that the only way to proceed with a railway was to quietly acquire the necessary land and make the line as their own undertaking and under their sole control. So this is what they proceeded to do and they managed, with some difficulty to buy enough land, by means of concluding several individual bargains with each owner. On 20th January, 1876 rail laying began, but with no official permission of concession rights for a railway.

Rapier's small narrow gauge steam engine, now tried, tested and proven in England, was given the name *Pioneer* and shipped to China in a packing case, all as originally intended. The Chinese have always

European and American visitors throng together on the first Chinese railway.

been skilful in carrying heavy loads by manual labour. However heavy the piece to be carried, its transport is only a matter of the skilful arrangement of bamboos, ropes and plenty of labour. So, *Pioneer*, weighing 26cwt empty, was carried by 16 men a distance of three furlongs without so much as pausing to draw breath. On 14th February, 1876 she made a trip on about three quarters of a mile of laid down track and so became the very first steam locomotive to run in China. The news was telegraphed to England: "Engine ran today. Chinese delighted."

The delight of the Chinese people was unbounded and they flocked daily to see the little engine at work. The Taotai of Shanghai viewed all this with great alarm and he became pressing with his demands to stop work. The company compromised by stopping work for a month but then carrying on unless definite instructions were received from Peking to desist. No instructions or further interference occurred and the company then made the next mistake of continuing construction on the basis there was no reason why they should not do so. The Chinese having been told to have nothing to do with the railway now flocked to see it in their thousands.

The *Times'* Shanghai correspondent wrote in May: "The engine, of course, is the great centre of attraction. It is engaged in dragging trucks with pebble ballast at present, and a general cry of "Laij tze, laij tze... it is coming... it is coming" heralds each return journey. Everything, therefore is going on so far satisfactorily. They are giving practical proof that there is no instinctive dislike in the masses to things foreign. Let us hope that this pioneer railway will get finished without further trouble, and that it will serve to introduce into China a mode of carriage which has done so much to develop the resources of western countries". All encouraging and logical western thinking, but without taking account of China's own views.

The first excursion train was run on 26th May, 1876. All continued to go well and the works were not interfered with. On 30th May the first permanent engine *Celestial Empire* arrived, was assembled and tested with a run to Kangwan running at 25 mph. A second engine named *Flowery Land* was delivered

later. Carriages arrived for first, second and third class passengers and on Saturday 1st July Chinese were invited to travel free on the railway and it was opened on 3rd July as far as Kangwan, five miles from Shanghai. The receipts were "at once of the most satisfactory character".

The good news did not last for long. Unfortunately a train knocked down a Chinese and, whilst the driver was acquitted of manslaughter as it appeared to be a suicide, the railway then became embroiled in a wider dispute and was closed for a while to seek to calm things down. This proved to be a mistake and gave the Chinese the upper hand they had probably been waiting for as they took the view that the Jardines' concession was for a road and not a railway laid on top of it.

The position was settled by an agreement that the provincial government should buy the railway with

---

WOOSUNG ROAD CO., LIMITED.

ON AND AFTER

MONDAY, JULY 3rd, 1876,

UNTIL FURTHER NOTICE, TRAINS WILL RUN ON THIS LINE

BETWEEN

SHANGHAI & KANGWAN

AS UNDER :—

Trains will leave Shanghai at

A.M.	A.M.	A.M.	P.M.	P.M.	P.M.
7	9	*11	*1	3	5

Trains will leave Kangwan at

A.M.	A.M.	A.M.	P.M.	P.M.	P.M.
7.30	9.30	*11.30	*1.30	3.30	6

FARES :

	SINGLE TICKET.		RETURN TICKET.
FIRST CLASS	\$0·50	..	\$1·00
SECOND CLASS, 300 Cash, or	0·25	..	600 Cash, or 0·50
THIRD CLASS, 120 Cash, or 10 for	1·00	..	200 Cash, or 6 for 1·00

The Full Number of Good Cash will be demanded. Children under 10 Years will be charged Half Fare.

The first railway timetable issued in China.

Ordinary service train at Woosung Creek station.

the price payable in instalments; until payment in full, the company could continue to work it and so the railway reopened on 1st December, this time for the whole distance to Woosung, but only for passengers as the Chinese refused to allow freight.

All proceeded well until the last instalment of the purchase price was due on 20th October, 1877; the final instalment was paid, ownership passed to the Chinese and the last train was run. Rapier himself summed up the outcome: "This is probably the first railway which has been completed, worked at a profit for twelve months, and then been bought and paid for in hard cash for the express purpose of stopping it."

The railway was taken up and a temple dedicated to the Queen of Heaven erected on the site of the Shanghai terminus. The popular story is that the rails were torn up and pitched into the Yangtze river. But there were persistent rumours that much of the equipment was retrieved and shipped back to Ipswich, so leading to the rumour that the coaches subsequently used on the three foot narrow gauge Southwold Railway to Halesworth originated from the Woosung Railway. This seems unlikely, but more plausible is the possibility that some of the track used to lay the Southwold Railway may have come back from Woosung and the coaches used at Southwold may have been intended for the Shanghai extension but never delivered. Intriguing theories to conclude an extraordinary story about how the British built an unauthorised Chinese railway and how the Chinese carefully but firmly dealt with the situation and removed it. The morale of the story is do not blindly believe your own logic will be recognised and accepted in the Celestial Empire or Flowery Land however pioneering and right it may seem.

> **This is probably the first railway which has been completed, worked at a profit for twelve months, and then been bought and paid for in hard cash for the express purpose of stopping it.**

The fabulous scene at Shanghai engine shed with *Celestial Empire* on the turntable and *Flowery Land* outside the shed.

The railway from NOWHERE

Over 70 British railway companies produced their own official postcards and the North Staffordshire Railway which operated the Leek & Manifold Railway was no exception and devoted eight of its 23 sets of cards to the line. This card features the NSR name on the picture and shows a train for Waterhouses approaching Thor's Cave station.

W hen one walks through the beautiful Manifold Valley today, along the path once used by the delightful 2'6" narrow gauge railway running past the intriguing Thor's Cave, it is difficult to conceive how such a railway would not be sought after by tourists and, possibly, even profitable if it was still running in the 21st century. Unfortunately, it is not running and there is not even a society aiming to re-instate it, unlike the much loved Lynton & Barnstaple line. The sad fact of life - or in the Leek & Manifold Railway's case - death, was that the line really ran from nowhere to nowhere.

The Manifold line was once largely sponsored by local people caught up in the railway mania who wanted a railway of their own. Its main passenger traffic did not originate from the locality. Even from the outset a large proportion of the traffic was foreseen as tourist day traffic. In practice the line could (and did) carry more traffic in one Stoke's Wakes Week than in a whole year, but this was not conducive to good accounting and profit-making and so, only eleven years after being absorbed into the London Midland & Scottish Railway in 1923, it succumbed.

Its stations were generally far from the villages they purported to serve and the potential extension to Buxton was not achieved; had it been, then we might have been faced with an entirely different outcome. Very probably its main line railway counterparts saw to it that such an extension never came to pass.

to NOWHERE

A train at Waterhouses station where the platforms were raised 6" above rail level to the height of the lower carriage steps. On the other side of the fence to the left was the North Staffordshire Railway's branch to Leek.

The authorisation and construction of the railway was made possible by The Light Railway Act passed in August, 1896 for the purpose of "facilitating the construction of light railways" which would be "found beneficial to the rural districts." The Act enabled Government and local authorities to provide financial assistance to railway promoters and for lines to be built as light railways under a Light Railway Order (so saving the costs of promoting a special Act of Parliament) with some construction concessions to reduce the capital cost in return for lower operating speeds to manage the safety risk.

Almost certainly, the special interest in the Leek & Manifold Railway comes from its engineer's approach. E.R. Calthrop came to the railway by chance. He was the consulting engineer for the Indian Barsi Light Railway of India built to the 2'6" gauge and had been asked by the Light Railway Commissioners, who were unimpressed by the scheme put forward for the Manifold valley line,

Wetton Mill Station, Manifold Valley, North Stafford Railway.

This second card shows a train at Wetton Mill station. The coloured card was derived from a photograph taken by Edwin Harrison the NSR's official photographer and used in the railway's set No.11. The cards varied in type, being collotype, photogravure and coloured photographs. In addition to being sent as souvenirs to friends, the railways used them as internal stationery for hotels, restaurant cars and refreshment rooms.

> **...the coaches were, unusual and startlingly, painted primrose yellow... a good colour match for the engines.**

to advise. Whilst Calthrop was making his report, the railway's engineer died and, as Calthrop had advised that considerable savings could be made in the execution of the railway works, he was asked to take up the engineers' mantle and did so to good effect.

Calthrop's view was that if light railways were to be developed in England, the narrow gauge was essential to obtain the full maximum advantage as regards cost. Actually, he went further than that and advocated in a paper delivered to the Institutite of Engineers in 1897 that a central organisation ought to be created to manage all the light railways in any one country so as to gain economies of scale. He stressed the need for standard components and rolling stock. To some extent he was advocating going further than the Board of Trade's light railway powers.

He reduced the construction estimate for the Leek & Manofold Railway by £11,000 by means of his patent system of adopting uniformity of axle

This shot shows the methodology of working with standard gauge wagons. A six wheeled milk van stands on a narrow gauge transporter at the end of a loading dock siding adjacent to a short section of standard gauge track at Ecton station, whilst the train has its single passenger carriage sandwiched by three transporter wagons, including a five plank open wagon all the way from the Southern Railway, together with two United Dairies milk tank wagons at the end of the train hauled by *E.R. Calthrop.*

W.H. Whitworth took this picture of a double headed train strengthened by transporter wagons having wooden seats and canvas canopies added. The train is at Hulme End in around 1918 and is probably a bank holiday working necessitating a second crew being sent out from Stoke to work the second engine.

load for all equipment, thus reducing the weight and so the cost of the track, adopting a maximum uniform load of five tons per axle to run on rails with a minimum weight of 30 lbs per yard at an ordinary speed of 15 mph.

The Leek & Manifold locomotives and carriages were almost carbon copies of the Barsi Light Railway. Maybe this was not surprising as that line too followed Calthrop's patent system, so savings would also have been made in adopting the same designs which were functional but also aesthetically beautiful as well as most probably being to a higher standard than usual for British light railways.

The two steam engines were handsome large 2-6-4Ts built by Manning Wardle of Leeds, the first of their wheel arrangment in Britain, and originally painted in an attractive chocolate brown livery ornately lined out. The coaches followed the Indian pattern and were, unusually and startlingly, painted primrose yellow, but which were a good colour match with the engines. They were unusually large bogie open saloons lit by electricity and with end balconies. At holiday times the original four carriages were insufficient and additional traffic was carried by fitting seats to the open goods and also the transporter wagons.

Calthrop continued with his innovations in relation to freight stock, tackling head on the issue of transhipment from standard gauge at Waterhouses

A.W. Croughton's picture of Hulme End shed on Saturday 22nd July, 1933 showing both engines, *E.R. Calthrop* outside the shed having been turned to face the other direction, after having been returned from overhaul at Crewe the wrong way round.

where an end on junction was made with the North Staffordshire Railway. He designed an ingenious transporter wagon which saved any unloading and reloading by the simple device of carrying the standard gauge wagon on a piggy back narrow gauge wagon. The only disadvantage was the need to build the railway's earthworks and bridges to standard gauge dimensions, so one wonders how much saving was actually made by constructing the line to narrow gauge bearing this in mind. These transporter wagons were the only ones of their type in Britain and proved most satisfactory and rode well at speed.

The transporter wagon

The wagon consisted of a narrow low steel body enclosing the bogies and the brake gear, with a platform 18" wide extending outwards from each of the lower edges of the body; in these platforms, which were 10" above the rails, were grooves to take the flanges of the standard gauge wagons riding on the transporter, their wheel treads resting on the narrow gauge wagon's platform. The standard gauge wagon was fixed on the narrow gauge transporter by an adjustable clamp surrounding each wheel. To enable the standard gauge wagons to be transferred onto the narrow gauge wagon, the transporter was run up to a low stop block at the end of a siding; beyond this was the standard gauge siding, the rails of which were at the same level as the transporter's platform. The standard gauge wagon was then run between the siding and the transporter either by man power or by using a capstan, the operation taking about 90 seconds. The various stations in the valley had standard gauge sidings so as to hold the wagons brought there by transporter. An ingenious system which would no doubt have had more general application to a network of narrow gauge lines connecting to an arterial standard gauge network.

A 1904 photograph of J.B. Earle in chocolate brown livery with a single coach train crossing the River Hamps between Waterhouses and Grinden; note the ladies on the footplate; one of four postcards issued for publicity.

A.W. Croughton took this shot at Hulme End station and shows the 1.25pm Wednesdays and Saturdays only train behind E.R.Calthrop on 11th July, 1928, with the engine then repainted in LMS red livery. Behind the engine on the transporter wagon is a coal wagon owned by Kirkland & Perkin, Buxton coal merchants who had a sales office in the goods yard at this station.

Calthrop's Manifold experiment is perhaps of more interest to the railway enthusiast for what did not happen but might have been. His patent design could easily have been a template for a wider application of the 2'6" gauge in Britain for light railways and rural lines rather than construction on the standard gauge. The Duke of Sutherland, on hearing the plaudits of the narrow gauge over dinner at the Oakley Arms Hotel on the occasion of Fairlie's double engine trials, wished he had spent less money by building narrow gauge railway in his Scottish highlands. One might imagine a network of narrow gauge minor lines constructed to the Calthrop design all over Britain. Great fun for the enthusiast but not really so practical or probably as long lasting. Transhipment of freight has always been a death knell to railways and a 2'6" gauge network would hardly have survived a Beeching axe if indeed it had lasted so long. Whilst India built an extensive metre gauge network, even that is now all in the process of either closure or conversion to broad gauge. So, the Calthrop experiment whilst interesting and effective from a text book view point, unfortunately turned out to be a white elephant, specifically so on the line it was developed for which ran from nowhere to nowhere. Most certainly the Leek & Manifold Railway is fondly remembered for the magnificent scenery around Thor's Cave, the beautiful large steam engines, the ornate and unusually liveried carriages and the interesting transporter wagons, but they did not generate the traffic to pay the bills and nor could they have done. There simply was not enough traffic. The LMS took little time in shutting its narrow gauge railway inheritance down. The line's equipment lives on mainly in model form which does not have to conform to the same economic criteria and can be enjoyed simply for its undeniable aesthetics.

This card shows the famous Thor's Cave and a train at the station of the same name. Whilst it has been coloured in, the primrose yellow carriages have been left in black & white. Note the tidy, well presented track, but the simple wooden station buildings.

Thor's Cave, Manifold Valley, North Stafford Railway.

BALDWINS
to the Rainbow

Jim Jarvis' shot of the classic Ashover Light Railway train: *Joan* in her second life at the end of the excursion day in Clay Cross yard with Hudson bogie wagons fitted out with seats. *Joan* was built by the Baldwin Locomotive Works in 1917 with their works number 44720 and named after Hermine Joan Carmichael Jackson. She was used during the railway's construction and then painted in crimson lake lined out in black & yellow with ALR on her cab sides (as can be seen in the picture). One never really knew which engine was which as the ALR used parts interchangeably: in 1948 when her left hand side tank developed a leak, a replacement tank was fitted from *Bridget* and so the engine became *Joan* on one side but *Bridget* on the other! When withdrawn, various of her part were used to keep *Peggy* serviceable for the last year or so.

AMBER VALE FROM THE BUTTS, ASHOVER.

We had come to Clay Cross on Sunday 24th August, 1947 with keen expectation, for the line was new to us. The train had been organised by the Birmingham Locomotive Club and was one of the first Society special trains to operate following the second world war at a cost for the day of just £9. The choice was excellent. We did not know it then, but ours was to be the very last excursion of all on the Ashover Light Railway from Clay Cross over the seven miles of grass grown track to Ashover Butts.

Joan stood sizzling quietly at the head of four open wagons, the whole ensemble dating back to trench warfare from the first world war. a former USA Baldwin 4-6-0T and English-built Hudson wagons. *Joan* was one of six identical engines bought from Army surplus to equip the railway when it opened. All the engines carried names from the railway chairman's family: *Hummy, Guy, Bridget, Peggy, Joan* and *Georgie*.

Before long, we crowded into the open wagons behind the very dirty *Joan*, her shrill whistle sounded and we jolted on our way, waved off by the very helpful manager: "The railway is yours for the day, come back when you like" he said.

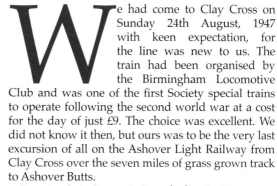

" The railway is yours for the day, come back when you like. "

The journey was a delightful one, for the route lay through a very pleasant part of Derbyshire and the weather was glorious. *Joan* acquitted herself well, clanking out of the yard and roaring up the 1 in 37 to cross the main Chesterfield road before reaching the open country and woodlands. While cameras clicked, water was taken at Fallgate, once a busy

A commercial tinted postcard showing Amber Vale from the Ashover Butts with the triangle in the foreground and an approaching one coach train in the distance. The Butts was a popular place for recreation, partly because it was one of the few level places in the Amber valley and, in local parlance, its name means just that: 'level area at the head of a valley'. One line of the triangle continued up the valley to Butts quarry and the passenger trains used to reverse out of the Butts station to turn on the triangle.

quarry yard with washing plant and screening mill. Then we climbed into the woods once more, behind the rocking and rolling *Joan*, throwing volumes of black smoke into the sky like a volcano as she wound her way through the valley of the River Amber towards Ashover. The terminus at the Butts lay some way from the village and was once the site for day excursions by train to the thoughtfully placed and intriguingly designed cafe 'Where the Rainbow Ends' with its octagonal roof painted to match its name. Although the ALR is long gone, the cafe survives reconstructed at Clay Cross as a sports pavilion; one of the remarkable survivors of a lost age.

Our return was a more leisurely affair, for shortly after leaving Fallgate we stopped before crossing a narrow road at Milltown, adjacent to the 'Miner's Arms'; the weather was far too warm to resist such a temptation, so all adjourned to the bar to slake

> ...speed appeared to increase after this stop, the wagons reeling along behind *Joan* rather like a string of drunken conga dancers.

thirsts. Our sojourn at the inn was to good purpose for, although the landlord was a bit 'took back' by this sudden avalanche of custom, he did us well with his limited supplies. We took the opportunity to grill the driver, Charlie Maycock, for reminiscences of the line and its locomotives. His yarns left us pretty uncertain which engine was *Guy* and which was *Georgie* due to the considerable interchange of parts between engines of the same design, or even whether *Georgie* had ever really existed as a working locomotive. We heard of the old days and the passenger service and how they had initially been such a success before the advent of the road motor bus after the first two years of the railway's life. After 1925, few regular passengers were carried but there was still a healthy local weekend

excursion traffic to the rainbow cafe, even to the extent that the railway obtained extra carriages from the Wembley Exhibition's 'Never-Stop' Railway. But, in 1936, passenger services had ceased entirely, by which time the railway had assumed a careworn look and the track especially left a good deal to be desired.

A passenger's eye view from the last excursion with the sun beating down from a cloudless sky on the enthusiastic passengers crowding in the rocking and roiling train, hanging on as best they could. The engine driver took no notice of the train rolling along but used it to his benefit to grab an apple from a tree in passing.

A.W. Croughton's picture shows Clay Cross yard on the morning of the excursion described in the essay with enthusiastic passengers, many dressed in jackets and ties crowding around *Joan* before the day's adventure. Some of those taking photographs are using second world war gas mask bags for their cameras. One participant proudly announced to his fellow passengers that he had taken photographs of *Joan* during the day in 23 different positions!

A Maurice Early shot of *Joan* on an afternoon passenger train approaching Ford loop in August 1932, when *Joan* was in more original condition, still with Baldwin stovepipe chimney and before the cab extension was added. After the first world war ended, some of the Army surplus equipment was stored at Purfleet in Essex and offered for sale by the War Stores Disposal Board in their magazine *Surplus*. General Jackson made an offer for four of the Baldwins at £1,000 a job lot which proved successful and they were delivered to Clay Cross in 1923.

An A.W. Croughton picture taken at Ashover Butts station on 23rd October, 1926 of *Joan* with a single coach passenger train. In the background are the ubiquitous Hudson bogie wagons standing in the coal wharf siding with a horse and cart behind them.

A renewed life came to the railway with the discovery of a local outcrop of coal near the line shortly after the war broke out, leading to a considerable amount of traffic towards Clay Cross, but this was short lived and, by 1942, the line was back to one daily train again.

History lesson over and refreshed, we climbed happily back into the wagons again to hang on tight as *Joan* lurched forward across the road. For some strange reason, speed appeared to increase after this stop, the wagons reeling along behind *Joan* rather like a string of drunken conga dancers. True to the Baldwin tradition, the old lady was eating fire as fast as she could, much of it pouring out of her stovepipe chimney, lighting the blackness of the smoke as it billowed over us, the cinders descending from the cloud as they reached the wagons causing many

> **"...the sight of *Joan* roaring, rearing, rolling and bucketing had to be seen to be believed."**

scorched trousers, but no-one cared for we were in holiday mood despite the supposed sombre occasion of riding the last train of all. The last two and a quarter miles from Stretton were covered in seemingly record time and the sight of *Joan* roaring, rearing, rolling and bucketing had to be seen too be believed. All too soon we were back again at Clay Cross and everything was quiet.

After this journey the line ceased to operate. The Railway Executive cancelled its order for limestone ballast from Ashover Quarry in January 1950. Its lifeblood taken away, the ALR closed at the end of that month. By then *Joan* had gone, for she was worn out and only *Peggy* survived to see the end, earning the doubtful distinction of outliving all the other narrow gauge Baldwins supplied for work in England.

FOOT NOTE

● Fortunately a small piece of *Peggy* has survived. PBW acquired one of her scratched and battered nameplates which our family and guests enjoy looking at nearly all the time.

Joan with the excursion train crossing one of the roads.

Marmalade sandwiches
and a flask of tea

Bottom left: **Bagnall 0-6-2T *Conqueror* at Ridham dock, Bowaters' system, on 21st September, 1960** Photo: Ken Cooper

Bottom middle: ***Scaldwell*, an 0-6-0WST built in 1916 by Peckett & Sons running on the ironstone system of the same name, photographed by Ken Cooper on 29th August, 1962.**

Bottom right: ***Nancy*, an Avonside 0-6-0T built in 1908 running on the Eastwell system, photographed by Ken Cooper on 18th April, 1956.**

E.S. Tonks wrote thirteen volumes about the Ironstone Quarries of the Midlands as well as many other pamphlets recording outline histories of narrow gauge industrial railways in Britain. Luckily he wrote down much of what we now know about the significant but fragmented industrial narrow gauge systems of Britain. His work was akin to the writings of James Boyd on the Welsh narrow gauge railways. Eric Tonks was a member of the Birmingham Locomotive Club which re-invented itself as the Industrial Railway Society and has gathered together much information about the systems it sets out to record.

Eric spent much time in the industrial world with his notebook and camera. Indeed, the early pages of his Northampton Ironstone work describes his happiness at his work accompanied by his marmalade sandwiches and his flask of tea!

In the Midlands of England there were many ironstone quarries stretching from Lincolnshire, through Leicestershire, Rutland and Northamptonshire to Oxfordshire. Most of the quarries were on high ground and connected to the main lines in the valleys by cable hauled inclines and their own railway line linking them to the national railway network. Whilst most were standard gauge, a few were built to narrow gauge and some used the very attractive steam engines built by Peckett & Sons of Bristol. The Scaldwell Ironstone Quarries were a

"The Furzebrook line had a lovely set of interesting steam engines all uniquely known by Latin numbers."

Above: **Bagnall 0-6-2T** *Superb* **of 1940 pauses on the Sittingbourne viaduct of the Bowaters Papermill Railway during shunting operations in the evening of 18th September, 1971** Photo: G.D.King

case in point. From the quarry, east of Brixworth, ran a three foot narrow gauge line for nearly two miles to the village of Scaldwell where the ironstone was transhipped into standard gauge wagons for the remaining journey to the main line at Lamport until the quarry closed in 1963. Scaldwell owned two Peckett 0-6-0STs twins built in 1913 called *Lamport* and *Scaldwell* and one Hudswell Clark 0-4-0ST built earlier in 1900 known as *Handyman*. The line also used 25 wooden side tipping wagons made on site and marshalled into two trains of nine wagons each.

The Loddington system interestingly ran two French built Corpet Louvet 0-6-0Ts, one of which, *Cambrai* built in 1888 was subsequently preserved outside the National Railway Museum at Tywyn for a while (and incongruously appeared adjacent to Talyllyn Railway trains) before moving on to the Irchester National

Nipper at Crewe
locomotive works.

Manning Wardle
Chevalier at
Sittingbourne,
Bowaters' system,
on 21st September,
1960 (Photo: Ken
Cooper)

Bagnall fireless
locomotive *Unique*
at Sittingbourne
(Photo: Ken Cooper)

Cambrai, one of two 'Corpet Louvet' French built 0-6-0Ts
in 1888 which ran on the Loddington metre gauge system,
but was then preserved firstly at the Narrow Gauge Railway
Museum, Towyn, and now at the Irchester Industrial Railway
Museum in Northamptonshire. Here seen in steam on 18th
April, 1956 photographed by Ken Cooper.

Railway Museum in Northamptonshire which aims
to recreate something of the former ironstone lines.
Several of the locomotives from the other ironstone
lines have also been preserved, including the
Scaldwell Peckett and, also, Kettering Furnaces No.3
can be seen at the National Trust's Penrhyn Castle
railway museum.

The Kettering Furnaces in Northamptonshire
dated from 1878 and had their own three foot gauge
tramway using Black Hawthorn and Manning Wardle
saddle tanks to transfer the ore from the quarries to
the furnaces. Wherever practical, the railway was
laid along the edge of fields so as to interfere with
agriculture as little as possible and the trains ran
through some three miles of countryside before
reaching the foundry. Here the railway adopted some
ingenious operating methods. Sidney Lelcux of the
Industrial Railway Society takes up the story: "The
section entering the works was on a gentle grade.
Here the 0-6-0T slowed with its train, uncoupled
but kept moving. Meanwhile the works shunter had
entered a short siding on the edge of the works. The
loaded train drifted down past this siding and then its
locomotive accelerated rapidly away from its train to
run out onto the furthest tipping dock road. As soon
as the last wagon of this train had cleared the short
siding points. the works shunter rushed out, chased
the loaded train and pushed it into the nearer tipping
dock. Such a burst of activity simply to save running
round was remarkable."

Further south on
the Isle of Purbeck
in Dorset ran a
delightful two
foot eight inch
gauge line owned
by Pike Brothers,
Fayle & Company

**As the forklift
truck had not yet
been invented,
a works narrow
gauge system
was developed.**

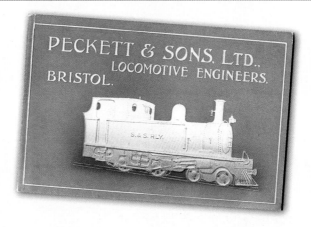

> **All seemed hopeless to continue but, at the eleventh hour, negotiations were successful to allow the railway to stay.**

which was popularly known as the Furzebrook Railway. This transported clay from the mines to the weathering beds and then on to the processing plant and storage depot at Furzebrook itself adjacent to the Southern Railway's branch to Swanage. The line had a lovely set of interesting steam engines, built by a range of well known companies including Peckett and Manning Wardle, all uniquely know by Latin numbers. *Secundus*, a unique steam engine built in Birmingham by Bellis & Seeking has been described in the last essay. *Septimus* features in a childhood drawing in the introduction!

Also in the south of England was - and still remains in part - the very last steam operated narrow gauge railway in Britain to serve industry, although it it now in preservation: the Sittingbourne & Kemsley Light Railway. There had been a paper mill at Sittingbourne since the 17th century with a short horse tramway to move goods up from the creek to the mill. The creek silted up, so a dock for deep water ships was constructed at Ridham to unload raw materials and load finished paper products. A 2'6" steam operated railway took the traffic up to the mill and back but this closed in 1969 and

Manning Wardle 0-6-0ST *Kettering Furnaces No.8* drawing a train of ore out of the quarry in August 1961. Photo: G.D.King

Quintus pauses briefly in the stillness of the woods near Creech Grange on a beautiful summer's morning in 1954 before proceeding on her way to Grange mine on Pike Bros' Furzebrook Railway.
Photo: Ivo Peters

1934 built Bagnall *Triumph* hauling one of the special trains to mark the closure of the Bowaters' system at Ridham dock on 4th September, 1969.

so all narrow gauge industrial steam came to an end in Britain, but not all was lost. Whilst some of the locomotives and equipment went to form the Great Whipsnade Railway, a lease of part of the line from Sittingbourne to Kemsley Down was granted to the Locomotive Club of Great Britain from 1970 and the steam engines entered the next phase of their usefulness running tourists over the line, including the unique concrete viaduct. The line was threatened with closure once again in 2008 when the Finnish company M-Real, who had taken over the paper mill, closed down operations and gave the steam railway notice to quit. All seemed hopeless to continue but, at the eleventh hour, negotiations were successful to allow the railway to stay and, recently, the land has changed hands again and the current owner is more sympathetic. Let us hope that this very last steam narrow gauge industrial system can re-invent itself and become sustainable to show future generations something of its purpose.

At one time, narrow gauge tracks could be found almost in every industrial complex so, in a publication of this type, only a flavour of some of the different type of lines can be given. Perhaps the best one to leave until last is the LNWR's Crewe works 18 inch gauge railway. Crewe works had raw materials arriving at one end and completed locomotives

The Eastwell iron ore cable way running down towards the agricultural flatlands, pictured by Ken Cooper on 29th May, 1958.

Narrow gauge wagons at Loddington Ironstone quarry photographed by Ken Cooper on 7th June, 1958 with his Zeiss Contaflex 35mm camera always used on a tripod. Ken was a fastidious photographer taking fabulous record pictures of industrial railway steam locomotives. Thank heavens he sometimes also photographed the general railway scene.

leaving from the other. As the fork lift truck had not yet been invented, a works narrow gauge system was developed by Locomotive Superintendent John Ramsbottom from 1862 to assist this transformation and an extensive set of tracks evolved around the works, with even a suspension bridge crossing the main line tracks so that the narrow gauge could reach the main line station.

The first steam engine for this system was completed in the works in 1862 and, appropriately enough, named *Tiny*. Four more were made and named *Pet*, *Nipper*, *Topsy* and *Midge*. *Pet* has been preserved and can be seen at the National Railway Museum in York, although for many years it was on display at the Towyn museum. Later, more engines were built under Webb's orders and, early in LMS days, a diesel was introduced but, on closure of the Crewe works system in 1932, it was transferred to Horwich works where the Lancashire & Yorkshire Railway had established a similar system using the same gauge.

Postscript...

'The railway press recorded the plight of the Sittingbourne & Kemsley Railway when it was given notice to quit. The press deplored the insensitivity of the paper mill owners who were hell bent on closing the last remaining steam hauled industrial railway system. That seemed to be that. I read the news with some alarm and, rather than just continue to turn the pages of the magazine, something made me reach for the phone. I then found myself leading a tricky negotiating meeting on behalf of the S&KLR with M-Real and convinced them not only to allow the railway to remain but also to donate some cash! Of course, such a position was not won just like that. The S&KLR had some legal rights which just needed pressing extremely hard and, as that is my day job, I did. Sometimes, it is good to use one's skills to help others in a less fortunate position. That is largely how much of the preserved narrow gauge railway network has come to survive...' MW

THE NATIONALISED NA

For some reason best known to itself the Great Western Railway persevered with the two Cambrian-owned narrow-gauge lines which it inherited after the 1923 Grouping of railways – it went even further and took over the Corris Railway in August 1930, although this was not so much a deliberate purchase as the result of an armistice with the Bristol Omnibus Company, who happened to own it. So it was no real surprise when the Vale of Rheidol narrow-gauge section was re-opened after the war. What was a little surprising was that this summer-only service began once again as early as July 1945; it was a refreshing change from the restrictions then in force in one form or another all over the country and the wartime slogan of 'Is your journey really necessary?' Unfortunately the services were slender in the extreme and around 1953-4 there

was talk in the valley that the lein bach was doomed; this must have reached those ears of authority also tuned to the apparent success of the revitalized Talyllyn Railway, and by the summer of 1955 changes for the better were evident. The locomotives were repainted and were presented with names, No. 7 becoming *Owain Glyndŵr* and No. 8 *Llewellyn*, whilst No. 9 regained the title *Prince of Wales*. The coaches, by then rather shabby in the faded County Donegal colours borrowed by BR, were restored to Great Western chocolate and cream, and for the first time for many years the service was improved to such an extent that trains were crossing at Aberffrwd. Even the exchange of tablets seemed to have taken on a new significance, for the old cane-and-pouch carriers used by the Cambrian were pensioned off and the light alloy Swindon patterns were used instead; but this was the result of replacing the old electric tablet

Prince of Wales runs up the Rheidol valley with the river in view below.

system by ordinary staff-and-ticket working for reasons of economy.

This happy state of affairs continued for a further two years culminating in some spectacular shuttle working between Aberystwyth and Llanbadarn for the Royal Welsh Agricultural Show, using an engine at each end of the train, whilst a Rover Scout camp held at Devil's Bridge as part of the World Jamboree celebrations ended on the last morning with a magnificent down train of eleven coaches.

From 1958 it became evident that if the line was to pay its way some considerable adjustments were needed, either to increase income or to cut working costs. These were

An aluminium BR double arrow logo adorns the cab side of No. 7: the three VofR locomotives were the only three steam engines ever to carry this insignia.

Above: **A.W. Croughton's picture of withdrawn No.1212 at Swindon works. She was replaced by a brand new No.9 and not rebuilt with a new number as was originally thought by historians; the GWR accountants designated the re-construction as a rebuild rather than a new engine so as to gain financial justification for the work.**

Left: **"Sold down the Rheidol"** is the slogan chalked on the smokebox of *Owain Glyndwr* as he stands at Devil's Bridge on the last day of BR operation in 1993; a team of BR employees working on the line had hoped to buy the railway but, instead, it was sold to a consortium of preservationists who already owned the Brecon Mountain Railway.

put into operation in the form of increased fares – which were still low by the standard that the public were paying on some other narrow-gauge lines – and by making economies. The simplest way of cutting operating costs was the old-established method of cutting services with little regard to the effect these cuts might have on revenue. So there were no trains at all at Easter, no more crossings at Aberffrwd, and the season began at Whitsuntide with only one train per day, ascending and returning in the afternoon leaving no time for tourists to visit the falls at Devils Bridge. In defence of BR it must be admitted that this one train had at times been loaded to seven bogies, the maximum load permitted for one engine. The service throughout the summer was varied, ranging from one train per day up to three at the peak season, and this variation had made it no longer possible to maintain regular crews for the section, the turn having become a regular one in the second main-line link at Aberystwyth.

Track maintenance was reduced, a gang of four men did the work previously carried out by eight, and no longer was there a dividing post in the woods of Cwm Seire; instead, a petrol trolley was now housed at Nantyronen and the morning patrol was done on this. Such economies were doubtless necessary, for the traffic season was by then woefully short leading to the future of the Rheidol being far from secure in these days of Beeching. However,

Above: **Tom Rolt inspecting No. 8 Llewellyn standing outside the GWR engine shed at Aberystwyth; even the water tower had been repainted in GWR colours.**

local political persuasion was effective and the then Minister of Transport, Barbara Castle, was prevailed upon to agree to keep the line open.

Once more an effort was made – British Rail repainted the entire fleet in house colours: rail blue! So, the gallant 2-6-2Ts continued their journeys to Devil's Bridge, clinging to the mountain side, sporting a blue livery with the infamous double arrow logo emblazoned on their side tanks. Actually, once they had been lined out in black and white and the nameplates given a red background they became tolerably smart.

And so the Vale of Rheidol survived the end of steam on British Rail, against all the odds. Who would have thought that in the 1970s, British Railways Board would still be operating three Great Western Railway built 2-6-2Ts!

More improvements were to come! Enthusiastic local management re-introduced some of the earlier colour schemes and even tried out some Cambrian Railway and original colours. No. 9 *Prince of Wales* was turned out in a startling yellow ochre livery with red frames, said to be the original VofR colour scheme. Whether it was or not it certainly caused a publicity stir.

For a gala, the local management turned to borrow an engine from the Ffestiniog Railway, recalling the heady days when England-built *Palmerston* was hired in times of need. *Palmerston* was sadly not available this time, but the FR lent a 2-6-2T of its own: an American Locomotive Company built first world war 2-6-2T, by then named *Mountaineer*.

All good things come to an end and, with the Government's privatization policy affecting the railway network, after 1993, the Vale of Rheidol railway was one of the first of the peripheral activities then sold off. Perhaps predictably, it was bought by experts already in the railway heritage business and joined their stable in company with the Brecon Mountain Railway. The local staff were miffed as they had hoped to do a management buy out. On a bitterly cold autumn day, the last Nationalisation trains ran with a chalked notice "Sold down the Rheidol" featuring on No. 7's smokebox door.

However, the new owners have set to with improvements and, despite a declining market, have refurbished and reconditioned most of the railway, cut down lineside trees to re-instate the valley view and the railway is in good heart. Great Western colours have re-appeared and coal firing has supplemented oil. Long may it continue.

Right: **Reflections on the Rheidol:** *Owain Glyndwr* hauls his train up the valley during the **BR blue era.**

Far right: *Owain Glyndwr's* **nameplate attractively picked out in red and set against the black & white lined background of the BR corporate blue livery.**

Above: *Owain Glyndwr* runs round his train at Devil's Bridge station in the mid 1950s. The line is fully signalled and staffed by BR(WR) men from Aberystwyth shed.

Above: *Prince of Wales* sporting the **BR** double arrow symbol hauls a train including one of the open coaches over the wooden trestle viaduct on the outskirts of Aberystwyth. (Photo: G.D. King)

Above: **For the 1982 season** *Prince of Wales* was repainted in 'original' **VofR** yellow ochre livery with red framing and cylinders, due to the enthusiastic local manager, David McIntosh, who was determined to increase the VofR's exposure to the market place.

Above: **No. 9** *Prince of Wales* poses at Devil's Bridge station, re-painted in full **BR** passenger engine lined green.

On 15th September, 1955 two trains stand in the narrow gauge station at Aberystwyth; on the left the 1.45pm train with *Owain Glyndwr* and on the right the 2.30pm train with *Llewellyn*. By this time, the carriage sets had been repainted in BR carmine & cream livery.

THE FARMERS'

Historical Notes
AND
Itinerary
in connection with the

LAST TRAIN
on the
WELSHPOOL and LLANFAIR LIGHT RAILWAY
on
3rd NOVEMBER, 1956

Organised by
THE STEPHENSON LOCOMOTIVE SOCIETY
(Midland Area)

The Stephenson Locomotive Society's black bordered brochure for the Last Train on 3rd November, 1956. All their brochures and many other early preserved railway publications were printed by W.J.Ray & Co. Ltd. of Wolverhampton.

The W&L in the last years of its working life. Llanfair station is still full of goods wagons as *The Earl* goes about shunting to make up the freight train for Welshpool.

The Talyllyn Railway was rescued from its coffin in 1951; the next funeral to be celebrated was at Welshpool five years later – the wake was quite a party, considering the W & L had done nothing but carry freight inconspicuously for 25 years. Although the Newtown Silver Prize Band struck up with 'Pomp and Circumstance' followed by the 'Dead March,' the centre of attraction was the elegantly polished and still active corpse, steaming away with over a hundred enthusiasts crammed into open wagons and both brake vans behind her. The wagon sides were locked in position with cotter pins by the station staff, Inspector George Holland passed the 'Right Away' to the driver and No. 822 *The Earl* with hissing cylinder cocks and a mushy exhaust, eased her train out of Welshpool yard. It was 3rd November, 1956.

On the opening day, 4th April, 1903, it had been *The Countess* which had been fêted – but otherwise the scene was similar even to the grey weather. *The Countess'* passengers had a more comfortable ride in the splendid clerestory-roofed bogie coaches, decorated fore and aft with the Prince of Wales feathers surrounded by leeks, whilst in white letters on the tank sides was picked out the motto: 'Success to the W&LLR'.

The Earl carried no slogan 53 years later, but both trains were cheered on their way through Welshpool and rocked by fusillades of fog-signals. The Stondart Quarry at Welshpool made their contribution to the 1903 festivities by detonating small charges of dynamite: but in 1956 this undertaking had already disappeared. At Llanfair the entire village turned out in the driving rain to welcome its first train, and amidst more fog-signal explosions the local brass band played *The Countess* in. Musical accompaniment was provided in 1956 by foreigners from Newtown nearly 20 miles away. They played *The Earl* out of Welshpool for the last time, then filed cheerfully into their motor-coach and lit up – it was a change from run-of-the-mill jobs anyway. Their coach

was the centre of some 50 cars and motor-bikes which followed *The Earl* to Llanfair. Like the first, the last train ran late, but this had no effect on the enthusiasm of the packed humanity in the open wagons.

Once past the exchange sidings and over the road *The Earl* began to cough her way up the bank over the canal bridge, and then slowed to a stand for the gated crossing over Church Street in the centre of the town, which was thronged with people. Here there was a legion of photographers and a jam of cars which had come to cheer the train and record its last journey. They stopped once again at Seven Stars to give the photographers a chance and then made their way up through the new housing estate, decked out with flags and streamers to greet the last run of the 'Llanfair Jinny'. Rejoining the road just short of Raven Square the train almost collided with the Newtown Silver Prize Band which had come up the main road on the other side of the town and was still blowing hard. All road traffic was at a standstill, for the photographers had abandoned their cars in every possible position including the middle of the road, to get their shots as *The Earl* crossed over Raven Square.

This was the beginning of the 'Great Chase', for as the train crept up the 1 in 46 towards Golfa a long queue of cars, including the Band's bus, kept funeral pace along the parallel road for as far as the eye could see. Every hedge, every gate, every field and every tree seemed to contain a photographer, and as *The Earl* slogged up the 1 in 29 and rounded the reverse curves even more photographers came charging across from cars abandoned on the roadside. Amidst the autumnal red, brown and green of the Welshpool countryside, 822 working flat out,

> **...I have much pleasure in declaring this line open and asking you to join me in wishing it every prosperity and continued life hereafter.**

LINE *opens, closes and re-opens*

On 4th June, 1953, *The Earl* waits patiently at Seven Stars, Welshpool as the engine crew bounce a car out of the way which is blocking the right of way.

breasted the first summit and the caterpillar-like train dropped over the other side with a clicketty-clicketty-clicketty and moved away from the road, the cars and the waving hands. The next stop was to be in the loop at Castle Caereinion and there were some lively debates in the open wagons as to whether the Band would make it in time, or be snarled in the traffic. They were late.

From Castle Caereinion, now away from the road, it was downhill again to the stone viaduct at Brynelin and here from the farms the local people came to wave. Then over the roller-coaster section and down to the waters' edge, the little train ran, over the moss-covered sleepers towards the steel girder bridge over the River Banwy, where the line levelled out. Beyond the water tank for the last mile the hordes of photographers came back into their own, and cameras were aimed from every conceivable vantage point in spite of the fact that the light was beginning to fail. Llanfair was entered with shrieking whistles and *The Earl*, now complete with 'Last Train' headboard, came to a halt beyond the ancient standard-gauge coach bodies used as stores and offices. The outward journey was over, the Newtown Prize Silver Band, which had finally caught up, played and 822 ran round her train, amongst a crowd of a size that Llanfair had not seen for many years.

Little time was lost in spite of them and, bunker first, *The Earl* set off for Welshpool, this time with even more customers on board for it was too dark now for effective photography and those with cameras were making the best of both worlds. The journey back was somehow quieter and more sombre for this was to be the very last run of all, and many of the passengers were not now feeling in holiday mood. This time there was no stop

at Castle Caereinion for there was little point, though spectators were there, as indeed they were at almost every accessible spot. At the stop board at the bottom of the bank from Golfa and alongside Raven Square the train came to a halt with a cloud of blue smoke showing from the brake blocks. By this time it had become quite dark and the queue of vehicles was readily picked out by the cars' lights. With whistle blowing *The Earl* crawled to a stop smack across the middle of Raven Square; the Band, which had come non-stop from Llanfair just to be sure, was ensconced on the roundabout giving all that it had under the light of the new tall concrete street lamps. The engine joined in the chorus, cars blew their horns and then the final stage of the run down to Welshpool station began. Whistles blew almost continuously as Inspector George Holland entered into the spirit of the occasion, flashlight bulbs lit up *The Earl* as she trundled

Early memories...

"If you look closely at the pictures of the Diamond Jubilee Re-Opening train in 1963 you may see a schoolboy with a red and green cap, blue mackintosh and wellington boots in the first compartment of the Chattenden & Upnor carriage. A friend and I had a whale of a day out on a narrow gauge railway we had never seen before. Of course, we had passed the track many times on the way to the Talyllyn, but as it was closed it was then of little interest to a small boy. Railways had to live and this one had started to do so again, so it gained my affection and, later in life, we lived near enough to it to for me to be able to learn to become a fireman on the 'GWR narrow gauge engines'."

down towards Seven Stars whistling again, this time for the road crossing with its uncountable number of cars snaking back to Raven Square. The Church Street crossing was also crowded with a sea of upturned faces, and as 822 came down towards the engine shed she was greeted by a shower of rockets and other fireworks.

Beyond the road in the station square, the excursionists climbed down from the brake vans and open wagons; some made their way to the main-line train which, though it was very late, had been held back specially, others hung around as *The Earl* pushed the wagons quickly back into the yard. The last day had come and gone.

On 6th April, 1963 the tables were turned. Sir Thomas Salt, Chairman of the new Welshpool & Llanfair Railway Preservation Society stood on a wagon in the station yard at Llanfair and addressed the crowd: "They say that history repeats itself. This is the Diamond Jubilee of the hour of the opening of the line 60 years ago by the then Earl of Powis." The Earl was invited to re-open the railway and did so with the following words: "It is a very great honour and pleasure to me to be invited because my family were intimately involved with the railway... the first sod was cut by my cousin, Lord Clive, in 1901 and he was presented with this spade as a memento of the event. I am sure you would be wishing to join with me to congratulate the members of the Welshpool & Llanfair Light Railway on the great project which they have now brought to fruition... they have got this railway back again through their very great efforts... I have much pleasure in declaring this line open and asking you to join me in wishing it every prosperity and continued life here-after."

The Earl then walked up to *The Countess* and drove her through a tape across the track, following which the train left for Welshpool to repeat history once again with a rather late luncheon at the Royal Oak Hotel.

The W&LRPS had been enormously lucky. Both of the original engines had been carefully stored away at Oswestry works under the watchful eye of Oliver Veltom in charge of the Cambrian division of BR, in the fervent hope that the preservation of the line would follow the successful revival of both the Talyllyn and Festiniog Railways, almost even before British Rail closed the railway in 1956. Whilst some of the original wagons remained, all the three carriages had long since gone; so some were acquired from the Navy's defunct Chattenden & Upnor Railway, fortuitously of the same 2'6" gauge, although these have subsequently been replaced with continental narrow gauge rolling stock; rather a pity really as the C&U carriages with the Planet diesel *Upnor Castle* (now part of the Ffestiniog Railway's dna) are real British narrow gauge equipment. Fine though the continental locomotives and carriages acquired by the W&L are, how much more appropriate it might have been for the line to have become the last bastion of the British 2'6" gauge. Ironically the C&U carriages have now found a home on the very last railway of such gauge to expire: the Bowaters paper mill system, although the W&L has retained a (so far) rather unsuccessful relationship with Bowaters' *Monarch*, the only 'Mallet' engine type ever built for the British Isles which currently resides on a plinth at Welshpool Raven Square Station, almost daring the preservationists to put it back into service. By good fortune, the W&L now has working replicas of all three of its original carriages and very fine they look too, running behind *The Earl* or *The Countess* and sometimes in mixed trains recreating the wonderful sight of a Great Western Railway narrow gauge train.

Intriguingly, exactly a year to the day before the re-opening, on 6th April, 1962 *The Earl* was lit up to go to fetch his sister *The Countess* which had arrived on a Flatrol

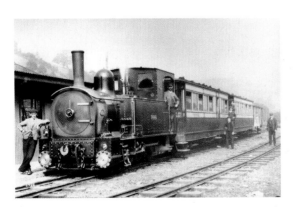

wagon in a pick up goods and shunted to the cattle dock for an overnight layover. *The Earl* arrived mid-morning and a fire was lit in *The Countess*. That day, the first for very many years, both original steam engines were in use on the railway together, both engines passing at Castle Caereinion station, possibly for the first time ever.

Whilst the re-opening specials were allowed to run the whole length of the line down to the Smithfield market, the use of the section of track eastbound of the Raven Square roundabout was short lived and soon dismantled. Although a town terminus and an interchange with the standard gauge Cambrian line would have been fun as well as preserving the integrity of the whole railway, this was not to be. A very awkward level crossing across the main street with absolutely no sight lines, followed by running through the middle of a housing estate and then across the busy Raven Square roundabout saw to the demise of that section. Whilst a very satisfactory new terminus has been built at Raven Square, easily accessible by the tourists who now arrive by car, several still turn a wistful eye to the closed town section with some regret. Regret increased by the relatively recent enquiry by Welshpool town to the preservation regime to see if they would be interested in bringing the railway back through the town section after all, but not taken up entirely for practical reasons. Maybe just a romantic dream, but it would have been a lovely idea to have re-instated the whole line. Maybe future generations will regret this never happened and one also wonders (rather like in the case of the Talyllyn Railway) whether those responsible for the custody of these lovely little railways are sometimes too pragmatic and too realistic. Surely preservation means just that. A true scheme would be to re-open the whole line and run it with original equipment. It is easy to make these comments in essays and I can feel the wrath of the current custodians of both lines, but I am unrepentant as the logic of rescuing these lines at all could quite easily be questioned. Just look what the Ffestiniog Railway has achieved in rebuilding the Welsh Highland Railway and what the probable long term outcome will be for the Lynton & Barnstaple Railway revival...

The modern day W&L on 25th August, 2001 with *The Earl* freshly restored with Heritage Lottery grant funds climbing up Golfa bank with a train of imported Austrian Zillertalbahn four wheel coaches - the front balconies of which are a fabulous way to experience the workings of the engine on the journey.

The scene at Llanfair Caereinion on the last day as *The Earl* rejoins the train for the farewell journey back to Welshpool, sporting two headboards. The Newtown Prize Silver Band are in the crowd.

Not interested in
THE CORRIS
at any price

Hughes No. 2 at Corris with a train of bogie carriages and all the station staff in about 1895. The station and its environs seem a little rudimentary and uncared for but the train is immaculate and the engine very clean, apart from the fireman's footsteps on the running board and some signs of priming water running down the stovepipe chimney. The photograph must have been taken for a special occasion but there are no details evident. Let's hope a reader can tell us of the event.

The Central Wales division of the Great Western Railway was run from Oswestry. Imagine the surprise when being informed in 1930 that their lords and masters had acquired the 2′3″ gauge line from Machynlleth to Corris! Of course, they knew little of the line, apart from its existence, but quickly set about finding out by memo - in those days most communication internally was undertaken by this means. On 29th August, 1930 the following urgent train message was sent to Mr. Hamer, the relief clerk at Machynlleth: "Will you please let me know by next train without fail, what is the normal position of the public level crossing gates on the Corris Branch, and also whether it is the practice to couple up the side chains on all stock, as well as the centre coupling."

Local management had to ascertain all the operating and commercial details of the Corris Railway itself, following acquisition of the line by the GWR for £1,000 as part of a wider (and much more important) deal to acquire the Bristol Tramways Company, which happened to own the Corris Railway. The GWR were interested in the BTC's bus interests in the City of Bristol and, in those days, there was no Competition Commission to stop them acquiring them as well as continuing to run the suburban trains. Indeed, the GWR owned quite a thriving road and bus network which it

used to advantage in connecting with its trains; it was not averse to withdrawing branch line passenger services and continuing to run the passenger services by bus if it felt it more economic to do so. The fact that the narrow gauge Corris Railway also operated its own bus services probably did not go unnoticed but, even though the GWR was interested in the bus operations of its parent company, it wasn't a foregone conclusion that it would buy the Corris Railway as well.

There had been several discussions between the GWR and the Corris before the BTC deal and a non-compete deal had been agreed in 1928 ensuring no conflict between the Corris' bus service between Aberystwyth and Machynlleth with the GWR's train service, also with no undercutting of fares. The Competition Commission would certainly be interested in such a deal today!

Intriguingly, the deal for the GWR was struck in just

The GWR was not interested in buying the Corris Railway at any price but, nevertheless did so for £1,000 as part of a wider bus deal in Bristol.

Above: **This has to be a publicity shot and was certainly used as a commercial postcard sold in Machynlleth**, probably taken about the time the bogie carriages were introduced into service, expediently using the former four-wheeled coaches and putting two on a new under frame. The Corris never ran double headed seven-coach trains in normal service, but here is one such train posed on the Dovey river bridge.

Top left: **The original station at Machynlleth in 1891** with an ornately lined out **No. 1** heading a train of two bogie carriages and a van. Passengers are all well dressed for an outing and pose for the camera.

Left: **No. 3** (now adorned with air pump on the side of the smokebox) standing under the trees at Maespoeth, back in steam on Corris metals again for the first time since 1948.

one meeting. It would have been very interesting to have been a fly on the wall then as the GWR started the meeting by making it clear that it was not interested in the Corris at any price, but by the end of the meeting agreeing to buy it for £1,000 at the same time as buying the Bristol bus company! Shades of an unwanted railway being offloaded at the same time as prize assets were for sale!

The GWR allowed the Corris passenger service to continue until the end of 1930 and then withdrew it, as the population in the Dulas valley opted for the bus which obligingly took them right into town, rather than the narrow gauge railway train which left them on the wrong side of the GWR station, itself on the edge of town.

The Corris Railway was then left to provide a rudimentary freight service, although the staff numbers were slimmed down. Whilst the GWR took great efforts to 'Great Westernise' the steam engines it acquired on its other two Welsh narrow gauge lines, it took no such steps with the Corris, despite both remaining engines visiting Swindon for overhaul.

The Corris had three original engines, Nos. 1, 2 & 3 all made by Hughes of Loughborough and a fourth of the standard 'Tattoo' type made by the Leeds firm of Hunslet. Nos. 1 and 2 were disposed of to a local scrapman, No. 3 went to Swindon in 1942 for an intermediate repair and the 'Tattoo' also received repairs as necessary. However, neither were given GWR number plates or safety valves and the railway was left to carry on much as it had always done.

The Corris Railway just survived into the nationalisation era on 1st January, 1948. It was then still too early to expect the slate trade to be re-invigorated after the war, although the slate extracted from the quarry at Aberllefenni were later to be good enough to be used at Heathrow airport. But the state of the River Dyfi was causing concern. Over the centuries it had often

changed its course and, now, further erosion was taking place between Machynlleth station and the railway river bridge. The newly formed Railway Executive did nothing to stop this and even moved the, by then, disused No. 4 down from Maespoeth shed just south of Corris to be stabled in the yard at Machynlleth, leaving the only remaining original Hughes built engine, No.3, to haul the remaining trains until final closure.

The last days of the Corris with No. 3 and a short goods train in Machynlleth yard in GWR days. Not much had changed from Corris days; the GWR had stamped its mark on the wagons but left the original Corris Railway number plates on the engine.

No. 3 on a passenger train at Aberllefenni in the 1920s. The circular plate covering the hole in the cab back sheet was removed when the fireman wanted to rake out the fire with one of the long fire irons.

business of a nationalised railway. Intriguing to think, nevertheless, what might have happened had the Corris and not the Talyllyn been saved for posterity. What if Tom Rolt had been ensnared by the charms of the Corris and its delightful passenger coaches running through the dappled sunlight of Fridd wood? Maybe one day we will still see this as the preservation society is going great guns from its small beginnings at Maespoeth engine shed in rebuilding the line, even with two recreated Corris steam engines. If both the Corris and the Talyllyn co-operated more to promote the region and joint long weekend trips, just maybe more visitors would holiday in the region to everyone's benefit all round.

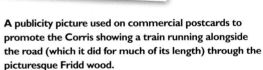

A publicity picture used on commercial postcards to promote the Corris showing a train running alongside the road (which it did for much of its length) through the picturesque Fridd wood.

> **The good fortune of the Talyllyn Railway should not be under estimated; it is highly likely that it would not have succeeded without the influx of two Corris Railway steam engines in reasonable order.**

The Dyfi river burst its banks over the weekend of 21st/22nd August, 1948 and Mr. Campbell Thomas, the Machynlleth station master took the decision to suspend the service. Although on 23rd August, the slide bars and piston rods of No. 3 had been oiled up for the day's work, this was not to be. Official confirmation of closure followed in September. The easy option to close had been taken and that was that. By chance, both the locomotives and all the wagons were at Machynlleth at the closure and so none had to be collected for disposal. Fortuitously, they were all available to help the nascent Talyllyn Railway Preservation Society get off the ground for, by extreme good fortune, both railways were of the same gauge - an enormous significance as the only other railway to the 2'3" gauge in the entire United Kingdom was the, by then, long defunct Campbeltown & Macrihanish Railway in Scotland. The good fortune of the Talyllyn Railway should not be under estimated; it is highly likely that the endeavours of that group of preservationists would not have succeeded without the ideal influx of two Corris Railway steam engines in reasonable order.

With hindsight, it was clear that the trackbed could have been repaired and stabilised and, had that been done, who knows how much longer the Corris Railway would have continued running, for it was in better condition than its neighbour the Talyllyn. But the closure decision was made and probably rightly as the line had become an anachronism and not part of the core

Footnote...

"We were on family holiday in Wales as usual over May bank holiday in 2003 and, as a bonus, we found that No. 3 and the TR's Corris carriage were to make their first visit to the railway since the line's closure. No. 3 had run in TR service that day and was taken to Maespoeth on a lorry and offloaded. We went to watch. I had the idea that the CR and TR staff would not be able to resist taking the short train up the line to Corris to try it out and so it proved. As bold as brass, I asked if my son, Stuart, and I could come along too and proffered a £10 note as a donation. The answer was "yes" and so we became the first fare paying passengers on the Corris since 1930!"

Perchance
it Waketh

No celebration about British narrow gauge railways could be complete without a story about the Lynton & Barnstaple Railway. The story of its closure makes a sad end to the railway's history, but the recent revival brings back hope. The recent construction of a brand new steam engine named *Lyd* after one of the local rivers (as was the practise of the original railway) and reconstruction of the railway from Woody Bay, restoration of carriages and now the construction of a second replica engine, the 'Yankee' *Lyn*, all bring some certainty to the challenge of reconstructing this railway, perhaps one of the best known of all the narrow gauge railways in the British Isles.

The railway has always had a place in the hearts of Devonians. It was an institution. The thought that the time might come when it would be no more was inconceivable. The possibility of closure simply did not exist in the minds of the locals. The line had become part of the holiday scene of North Devon. But, when it came to using the railway themselves, unfortunately it was a different matter. Consequently, after the short months of the holiday season, there were long months of comparatively

meagre traffic which did not please the Directors of the Southern Railway owners at all.

The announcement of the closure was a shock, a big shock, to the local people and indignation against the Southern Railway ran high, for the company was adamant about its decision. The Railway said they had been losing over £5,000 on the line each year for some years and that they had also supplied a brand new engine, overhauled the others, improved and reupholstered the coaches, re-sleepered the track, improved the fences, installed new signals and station accommodation and bettered the train service. Yet, even then, the locals did not use the railway; so why should the SR continue to operate it at a loss? What a pity that the concept of the railway preservation society had not then been invented!

The summer service of 1935 was the railway's last. The Southern Railway had remained unimpressed by the deputations and appeals. At one meeting, the Lynton delegates had come by car, because they said it was more convenient. Words could not hold much meaning after that.

The last train ran on Sunday 29th September, 1935. It was a public excursion hauled appropriately by *Yeo* and *Lew*, the first and last

The opening of the railway on 11th May, 1898 with the first train at Lynton. "The railway was declared open to the public by Sir George and Lady Newnes, amid scenes of great festivity, large crowds gathering at stations to welcome the first train which, of course, was decorated with flags, whilst Lynton itself was gay with banners and emblems of goodwill."

Right: **The last train was hauled appropriately by Yeo and Lew, the first and last engines supplied to the line. Here, the two engines sit side by side on shed in Pilton yard before moving off to haul the last train on Sunday 29th September, 1935.**

Below: **Commercial postcard of the L&B with a train on Parracombe bank. Part of the handwritten note on the reverse reads: "Have been here at Lynton today. Lovely country and sea scenery. Changed at Barnstaple onto this funny little railway..."**

family albums up and down the country.

The double-headed train steamed out from Barnstaple into the sunshine with whistles sounding defiantly for more than a mile, whilst several hundred people had assembled on the North Walk to watch the departure. Everywhere along the route stood old friends of the railway, there to say farewell to *Yeo* and to *Lew* making this, their last journey. Even in the fields, shepherds paused to give a wave of their hand and at one point a farmer held up a horseshoe. Through the woods ran the little train with its green engines and coaches, through the steep cuttings already coloured with the first bronze of autumn, and over the 70ft high viaduct at Chelfham, there to wait a while to take on water, each engine in her turn. Then the train ran on northwards, following the green valley, through deep rock cuttings and dense woods, round winding curves to Bratton Fleming, then through more rock cuttings and over more serpentine curves and steep gradients to Blackmoor, before descending to Parracombe Halt for water again. Then through the heather-covered fields its route lay, to the moorland summit at Woody Bay, 980ft above sea level, and finally the long descent, by deep rock cuttings and hillsides commanding magnificent views, to Lynton, where the train was ceremonially met by the Chairman of the Council, supported by a large crowd.

On these occasions it is always the homeward journey which is the sadder, for on the outward there is inevitably the feeling that this is not finality, that there is at least one more run to make. This was no exception. All too soon the green of the guard's lamp flickered for a moment at the end

engines supplied to the line. The weather was fair and over three hundred people turned up to travel on the train and witness the last rites. The reasons for their making the journey were varied; among the crowd, local people had come to say farewell to an old and faithful friend, for there were many of them who truly regarded it as such and some of whom had even seen the railway opened. Others came as railway enthusiasts to make a last pilgrimage, while for the majority, the distinction of travelling on the last train was a good excuse for having a day out.

There was no official ceremony, though the guard wore a sprig of rosemary as a token of remembrance. Generally, it was a happy party, but there were still some who had little joy in their hearts as they set off on the last journey to Lynton. As has been the case in so many last runs which have followed, it was a gala day for photographers and records of the day must surely be found in

Yeo and Lew with the last train standing in Pilton yard before leaving on their final return journey from Barnstaple.

The 'Yankee' Baldwin-built 2-4-2T *Lyn* at Parracombe. During the first year of the railway's operation it was found that a fourth engine was needed and, because there was then an engineering strike in England, an order was placed with the Baldwin Engineering Works in Philadelphia, USA, who built and delivered this engine at very short notice.

Many local people had come to say farewell to an old and faithful friend at Barnstaple Junction. Here they crowd round and on the two Manning Wardle 2-6-2Ts *Yeo* and *Lew* before the train leaves for Lynton.

of Lynton station platform and the train slowly moved out into the gathering darkness, with the two whistles of the engines sounding in shrieking chorus, detonators exploding and the town band playing 'Auld Lang Syne'. All Lynton seemed to have turned out for the occasion and somewhere 'The Last Post' was sounded. Far down the crowded train the chorus of song was taken up to the music of the band, who had insisted on travelling as far as Blackmoor, the Chairman of the Council and several others making this short journey their last. By now the weather had begun to deteriorate into a steady drizzle and, with the darkness, the scene became dismal in the extreme,

though the spirits of the cheering crowds remained un-dampened as station after station was left behind, detonators exploding on each occasion.

Toward the end of the journey, there was some anxiety on the footplates, for the prolonged whistling when approaching and leaving stations had taken a toll of steam and water so that the engines' tanks were getting low. They came home to Barnstaple shortly after 9.40pm, crawling round the curve within sight of the windswept Taw to meet a large crowd of almost a thousand people who, in spite of the downpour of rain, had begun to gather as early as 9.00pm outside the Town Station. Barnstaple, too, had come to say goodbye.

A.W.Croughton's portrait of *Lew* at Lynton with the 11.00 am train for Barnstaple on 13th October, 1926.

FAIR DAYS ONLY

The last days of the most westerly narrow gauge railway in the British Isles

THE TRALEE & DINGLE RAILWAY

The Tralee & Dingle Railway was a classic and much-loved three foot narrow-gauge railway built to open up a rural and defiant part of Southern Ireland. As with all such lines, the advent of motor transport sounded the death knell. The First World War saw the beginning of the decline. The end of hostilities did not bring an end to the difficulties for it was not long before the 'troubles' began. The Tralee & Dingle was in the heart of the Sinn Fein country and the locals were great sympathisers. The Sinn Fein on occasion would send ammunition to Dingle hidden under coal in the engines' bunkers, and it was the guard's flag which conveyed this information to an apparently uninterested passer-by.

Often the men were told nothing about it and their first intimation was when the contact at Dingle came along to collect.

After the amalgamation with the Great Southern, life became much quieter. The 'troubles' were over and everyone was anxious to lead a normal life. The railway was still an important link with Dingle and the roads were as yet unmetalled and quite unsuitable for heavy traffic. The years that followed saw more and more of the population of Western Ireland emigrating, thus reversing the original purpose of the railway, and gradually the traffic declined. Early in 1939 the road to Dingle was properly surfaced with tarmacadam and this, coupled with the fact that if passenger services were to continue to run, the permanent way would have to be entirely renewed, brought about their suspension.

A daily goods continued to work down to Dingle until 1947, when a national fuel shortage caused this last service to come to an end. Thereafter trains were run only on the occasion of Dingle Fair which took place on the last Saturday of the month, the empty stock being run down on the previous Friday. It was obvious that this could not be economic and the line shut for all time on 22 July 1953.

But it was whilst life hung by just this single thread that the Tralee & Dingle became known to the world at large, for the journey was perhaps the last piece of adventurous railroading to be found in these Islands.

It was possible to travel on this special train, but not before signing a stamped indemnity against CIE's liability for injury and paying for a return ticket at road bus fare. The 'Special Traffic Notice' read that the train would leave at 11.00am on the last Friday of the month,

A very rare early Tralee & Dingle picture (taken from a newspaper block), considered to be a scene at Tralee station in 1890 on one of the pre-opening inspection visits made by Colonel Hutchinson, the Board of trade Inspector or, possibly, a pre-opening 'look see' joy ride by the railway's directors.

> **The Sinn Fein on occasion would send ammunition to Dingle hidden under coal in the engines' bunkers, and it was the guard's flag which conveyed this information to an apparently uninterested passer-by.**

The cover picture of PBW's *Narrow Gauge Album* and a picture of which he was justly proud depicting 1T and 2T nearing the summit in June 1950. We have 16m cine film of the same train which was taken by my mother!

Jim Jarvis' shot of
6T on the Cavan
& Leitram's
Arigna branch.

but in actual fact this was never so for the crew were not prepared to spend a night in Dingle until they had been paid.

During the latter part of the summer the cattle traffic was heaviest, for by then the sparse amount of grass around Dingle had been eaten and the animals were sent to the more succulent feeding grounds of the Midlands for fattening. Until the very last years there were four engines left at Tralee, Nos 1, 2, 6 and 8 and for the monthly trip all four had to be steamed, each train needing to be double-headed over the steep banks. Later when No. 6 went to the West Clare, this loco shortage had grave disadvantages. It was at such a time that they lost a chimney.

This happened to No. 2, which had been left for a time with her chimney under a hole in the shed roof at Tralee; and the occasion certainly dates from the time when they had enough wagons for two double-headed specials, or maybe two double-heading and another, but only three engines. It was early autumn and the rail was bad, mists and damp grass making life very difficult. So the engine concerned left Dingle assisting the first special in the morning, and they ran out of sand and got stuck. This meant that Garret, the loco foreman at Tralee, had to go out to them with a lorry and more sand. Finally the engine was going back to Dingle on its own, bunker first, to get the last train out, and it was now dark. Anyway it was quite late at night when Garret's phone rang again – it was the station-master at Dingle.

'The engine has lost its chimney and the driver wants to know what to do.'

'Impossible. You must have got it wrong. Get me the driver.' So he was fetched.

'When I got back here the chimney was gone – what will I do?'

'Nothing I can do about it, come home the best you can.'

So he set out gingerly from Dingle with the train, and sure enough a couple of miles out, there was the chimney lying between the rails. They picked it up and threw it on the front, and she steamed all right – but they ran out of sand again. Anyway they were in Tralee just about in time for Mass on Sunday morning.

But to get back to the story. About 10.30am Tralee came to life, the engines were eased out of the shed, between rows of derelict drab grey cattle wagons, and run down to the padlocked turn-table. If the key could be found quickly all was well, but often the fireman was sent running for a hacksaw. Then after moving the odd car parked on the track they would run in turn down the street to the island platform in the main goods-yard for coaling. The small bunkers were probably all full of briquettes, so the cab floor, the fireman's corner and the front platform were piled high by the loaders, for enough had to be carried for the round trip and more. Then with the bell on the boiler-top ringing, they would return with a brake van to pick up the dwindling rake of serviceable vehicles for the special. All stock was provided with the automatic vacuum brake – a very necessary fitting in view of the gradient profiles – and centre couplers of the normal 'chopper' type.

As far as was possible the section was worked by old Tralee & Dingle men, and certainly by Great Southern men who had worked the line before – normal broad-gauge men could not be bribed into doing it. On balance, one's sympathies lie with the broad-gauge men. The only remaining true T & D man was Paddy O'Hanlon who worked the trip regularly and whose home was still at Dingle, 31 miles from his place of work.

The maximum load was 18, made up of 17 cattle vans and one ex-passenger brake van, now converted into part cattle wagon, part guard's van. This was adapted by the erection of a crude waist-high partition protecting the

Postcard of the 'last train out' of Castlegregory station in April 1939.

crew from too intimate an association with the livestock. At least one such van had the handbrake screw smack in the middle of the cattle portion. On discovering this the language of any non-Dingle man who got shanghaied into this job had to be heard to be believed. 'Would you be telling me now,' he said, 'how the _____ ing hell I'm to get at the b_____ brake with all them _____ cows.'

A ride on the footplate of the leading engine was probably one of the most worthwhile railway experiences any amateur could have. Departure would usually be around noon, and as the whistle answered whistle the locomotives drew away with a clank of coupling rods in a cloud of steam from open cylinder drain cocks. Looking back one would see the cheery wave of the guard's hand which showed that he had survived the snatch and that his van was still attached to the train; and so the journey began.

The line set out from Tralee in an unassuming fashion, writhing round back gardens and over four level-crossings before reaching the open country at literally sea-level, by the old Tralee Basin Halt. Here the waters of the marshy estuary of the River Lee have been known to flood the track, for the dykes of this tidal river have been broken down never to be repaired, since no-one was anxious to accept the responsibility for the repair of the river bank, especially as the breach provided an alternative area for the flood water, keeping it away from the lower part of Tralee. On occasions of high spring tides, trains had to wait several hours for the flood to subside, though more venturesome and less patient drivers have had their fires put out.

> **Looking back one would see the cheery wave of the guard's hand which showed that he had survived the snatch and that his van was still attached to the train; and so the journey began.**

Beyond the Basin on the left rose the mountains of the Slieve Mish, crowned by 3,127ft. Mount Brandon. To the right lay Tralee Bay, azure beneath a clear summer sky. So without much exceeding 15mph the train ran gently to Blennerville, where the line disappeared between two rows of houses, across the village street and up an alley no more than ten feet wide before bustling out on a sweeping curve to join the Dingle road. This first section followed the road in true tramway style, avoiding no undulations or bends and occasionally swinging across in startling fashion from one side to the other. Motorists needed their wits about them for there were no crossing gates and trains did not slacken speed. There were the usual scenes of alarm and excitement when horses or other straying livestock were encountered – some apparently bent on suicide. The usual way of dealing with this was by shouts, loud whistles and wild gestures from both ends of the train, but if all else failed the fireman would climb up on to the coal bunker lid and pelt the offenders with briquettes.

Forty minutes out of Tralee the signals of Castlegregory Junction came into sight – pulled off by 'Paddy' the general factotum for a non-existent special in the opposite direction. By the time the train had clanked to a stop the fireman of the leading engine would be out on the tank top ready to drop the 'bag' in, for, as everyone knew, time was of the essence during the scheduled ten minutes allowed, so that engines and men could get a drink. All were expected to join Paddy in a good glass of porter at Fitzgerald's bar over the road, and never was a bar so well placed.

An A.W. Croughton shot of a Catlegregory train at Castlegregory Junction with 2-6-0T No. 3T. The Great Southern Railway added suffix letters to all narrow gauge engines they took over. The T suffix, of course, signifying the Tralee & Dingle Railway.

A lovely shot of my Mother and Ivo's Bentley in June 1950 at Skirlough road crossing with 1T and 2T beginning the climb of Glenagalt bank, at 1 in 29, the stiffest (and longest!) banks on any railways in these Islands.

Soon both safety-valves would lift in a deafening roar, for these little engines were never short of steam. Shortly the crew would return to begin the battle, for whilst the line from Tralee was undulating and twisty, the line westwards was of a very different character. Once the junction was left behind the fight against nature began, for the train stood at the foot of the celebrated Glenagalt Bank, certainly the most formidable in Ireland and probably unsurpassed in length and severity anywhere in the British Isles. The rails climbed from almost sea-level to a height of 680 feet in just under four miles, with ruling gradients of 1 in 30 and 1 in 31. It was bad enough when maintenance was good, but with the grass lying over the rails life often became difficult in the extreme.

It would be 1.00pm before the new train staff for the section to Annascaul was collected, and 45 per cent cut-off with full regulator was the rule on Glenagalt. Once more whistle answered whistle and two smoke-stacks erupted smoke and steam simultaneously like miniature volcanoes. Speed varied between 5 and 15mph depending on the adhesion and, accompanied by the slow syncopated rhythm of the two locomotives, the train set off on stage two of its journey.

Not far from Castlegregory Junction was a steel bridge set upon a most acute semi-circular curve, close to the spot where once there was an even steeper grade and a more vicious curve, abandoned as the result of an accident when a mixed train from Dingle ran away from the summit and plunged from the rails into the gully 50 feet below. Drivers would never hesitate to point this out gleefully with complete disregard for one's peace of mind, especially in the return direction. This spot marked

> **Time was of the essence during the scheduled ten minutes allowed, so that engines and men could get a drink. All were expected to join Paddy in a good glass of porter at Fitzgerald's bar over the road, and never was a bar so well placed.**

the beginning of the real climb – 1 in 31 alongside the Dingle road.

From here there was yet another hazard to be encountered – stray sheep. These were dealt with by whistling, ringing and opening the cylinder cocks, and after a short chase most of them would scramble through the dilapidated wire fence to the valley below. By this time the train had slowed almost to a walking pace and the fireman put on another four or five shovelfuls of broken briquettes and dust, the little engine laying a smoke pall over the bare hillside, deathly silent save for the labouring exhausts. Down in the valley Paddy O'Hanlon pointed out the lonely farm house on the side of the spring of Gleann na Galt, the place of the mad, to whose waters was attributed magical powers in the healing of simple minds. Then in a final flurry of smoke the train leveled off in the little cutting at Glenagalt platform, dived under the road bridge and the engines shut off steam.

From here the line twisted and turned following each indentation in the hillside and all the time descending in long stretches of 1 in 29-30. Footplate passengers glanced at the vacuum brake for reassurance, remembering the fitter back at Tralee tinkering with the hose coupling rubbers to cure the worst of the leakage. As the train came snaking down the hill with the weather-beaten cattle trucks wagging wildly there was still the sheep hazard to contend with and this was met by firm brake applications, open drain-cocks and the squeal of flanges. The temporary panic over, then gravity once more took charge and the train bowled down the bank at 25-30 mph, the engines nosing their way along the rusty grass-grown track. One thought quickly of the four men employed to maintain these 31 miles of narrow-gauge track, and tried to keep this out of one's mind. Soon the line came into Gleann an Scail, where the legendary hero Cuchulainn fought his great battle with the giant, and the countryside is strewn with the rocks they hurled in their combat. With a long whistle the leading engine shot across the road at a blind and unprotected crossing, under an arch of trees whose branches brushed the cab roof, and dropped down into the station at Annascaul.

Here again men and machines took refreshment, but alas the village bar was too far for a visit. But all was not lost, for here was yet another factotum sent down by bus from Tralee for the weekend. He had obtained the requisite bottles. The water point for the engines lay beyond the station level-crossing at the Dingle end of the yard, so by the time both engines had been watered and pleasantries exchanged, a minor traffic jam of lorries and donkey-carts was in evidence on the road. But this was of no importance.

The fireman took a long swig from his can, mopped his brow and proceeded to lay a smoke-screen over the twelve-feet high fuchsia hedges in readiness for the long slog up to Garrynadur. The driver having been round his engine and found all well despite the coating of grass on the motion, whistled up; the driver of the train engine pulled on his whistle cord too, and then the train set off to face a second long climb with occasional glimpses of the blue water of Dingle Bay between the coastal hills. Up here the track seemed less overgrown with sharp exhausts and rhythmic kicks of the reversing wheel against its securing chain, the

engines made good progress up the bank to the grassy platform at Garrynadur. Here was the ganger's house and the probable explanation for the better track, but after a wave from the ganger's daughter the train was off on a repetition of the descent from Glenagalt until the grinding brakes brought it to a stop on the last few yards of the 1 in 29 at Lispole, close to another deviation made to ease curvature after a serious derailment.

Just ahead lay Lispole Viaduct – the line's major engineering work; a spidery steel two-span structure with stone approach arches. The 1 in 29 finished at the start of the steel spans. Light construction and 60 years of salt-laden breezes off the Atlantic had taken their toll, and in later years two engines were prohibited from crossing the viaduct coupled. This edict was usually honoured in the observance on the outward journey, but in the breach on the return. However, anyone standing on the wooden decking as the train ran over at walking pace would have his sympathies entirely with the civil engineer.

Five more miles of undulating track were yet to come before the final terminus was reached. A mile of this from Lispole was almost dead straight, and road and rail ran parallel. This section was taken under easy steam, galloping along at up to 25mph with friendly waves from cars and farm carts. Then, with the sweep of Dingle Bay in view on the left and beyond the blue-grey mountains of the Waterville peninsula, the grade stiffened; with a howl on the whistle the leading engine suddenly swung left across the road as it turned and dived into a narrow passage, almost scraping the low stone wall separating rail from road and elbowing the hedge on the left. Here the grass lay deep on the track and the bottom corner of the motion plate cut a swathe in the vegetation. The pilot engine shook with the violence of the slipping which resulted, while the fireman patiently tugged at his sanding handle. The train engine too began to slip, and with the train itself gripped by the curve the whole came to a noisy stand. They set back, the fireman sanding continuously, and had a second try, but got scarcely a yard beyond

the previous limit before they stalled again. Paddy's fireman climbed down and laid a thick carpet of sand on each rail, standing on the pilot as they set back again – that large box of sand on the front of the running plate was no ornament. This time, accompanied by billowing smoke and a tattoo from the train engine they finally made it, the rails dipped and they coasted down at the roadside until the wood and concrete barn-like structure of Dingle station with its two guardian signals, came into sight. Behind the yard lay the land-locked harbour, fishing boats loafing against the quay, answering with its tranquility our furious efforts to reach it. At 3.30pm we came to journey's end, to the most westerly rails in Europe.

The last train to Dingle: 2-6-0T No. 8T with train crew posing at Tralee station on 22nd July, 1953.
Photo T. O'Brien

Early memories...

"I sort of made a visit to the T&D but sadly not in a form I will ever remember as I was 'en ventre ma mere'. But my Mother still regails the adventures of the age, chasing the Dingle train, taking movie and black & white pictures when PBW couldn't manage both at once and, also, great dinners in Tralee with Ian and Molly Allan before ABCs were invented. We have a super short colour cine film entitled *Fair Days Only* of one of the last years taken by PBW using his grandmother's clockwork 16mm camera: a precursor to *Railway Roundabout* yet to come."

Tralee & Dingle Railway gradient profile showing Glenagalt as the high spot on the line.

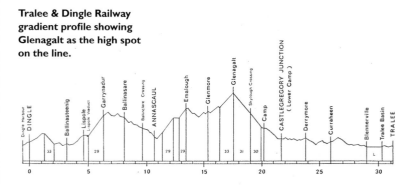

RED BALTIC TANKS
on Bank Holiday specials

THE COUNTY DONEGAL RAILWAY'S INDIAN SUMMER

A narrow gauge scene to die for today! 2-6-4T *Drumboe* and 4-6-4T *Erne* at Londonderry on 29th June, 1939 waiting to leave with special trains run in connection with the Northern Counties Committee Portrush excursions.

Blanche **on Donegal turntable.**

Those in search of Irish narrow-gauge networks had to trek northwards to Donegal. Here there were two railways of some size, connected together by a direct spur at Letterkenny and the Port & Harbour Commissioners' line at Londonderry. They were the Londonderry & Lough Swilly Railway and the County Donegal Railways Joint Committee. The former rejected transport by rail, embarked on the purchase of buses, bought out competitors and eventually replaced all its railway workings by motor road services. The latter, probably because it was jointly owned by two large railway companies (the Great Northern of Ireland and the LMS), decided that it could best serve the public by the introduction of what were virtually rail buses to suit the local needs. The Donegal also had the advantage that its stations were relatively close to the villages it served whereas this was not the case with the Lough Swilly Company. Even as late as the 1950s it was a relief to turn from the spectacle of closed and dying narrow-gauge railways to the bustling and efficient County Donegal Railways Joint Committee with its route mileage still verging on 100.

In other ways too the Donegal seemed to have the edge over the others. It had, in its later days, glorious red engines complete with superheaters, steam sanders and both steam and vacuum brakes which it kept in working order for as long as trains ran. True, the Cavan & Leitrim section of the CIE kept going entirely with steam, but this

was a last despairing effort at the behest of authority over 100 miles away which cared little for the condition of the locomotives so long as the coal traffic was cleared. The Donegal was in full and reliable operation to the end, and proud of it. Admittedly the West Clare was this too, but with the disappearance of steam its glamour went and it became somehow a shadow of its former self.

In all, the Donegal owned 23 steam locomotives, seven of which were in service when railway operations ceased. They were of five classes, beginning with three Sharp Stewart 2-4-0s built for the opening of the West Donegal Railway in 1881 and named *Alice*, *Lydia* and *Blanche*, after members of the Lifford family. In 1893 there followed Class 2, comprising six engines, all 4-6-0 tanks; these were built by Neilsons and were, No. 4 *Meenglas*, No. 5 *Drumboe*, No. 6 *Inver*, No. 7 *Finn*, No. 8 *Foyle* and No. 9 *Columbkille*. For some reason unknown to the author the company ordered two 4-4-4 tanks (Nos 10 and 11), again from Neilsons, and these were delivered in 1902; they were the only engines of this wheel arrangement ever to run in Ireland and they were named after the chairman, Sir James Musgrave and Hercules Hayes, a director. These three early classes were all scrapped by 1937, the 4-6-0 tanks outliving the others as a class by four years.

The remaining three classes were represented to the end and all were built by Nasmyth Wilson. No. 12 *Eske*, No. 13 *Owenea*, No. 14 *Erne* and No. 15 *Mourne* were all 4-6-4 tanks and were named after rivers in Donegal. They were renumbered 9 to 12 in 1937 and all four engines were fitted with Livesey superheaters. Class 5 consisted of five engines, all 2-6-4 tanks, built between 1907 and 1908. They were No. 16 *Donegal*, No. 17 *Glenties*, No. 18 *Killybegs*, No. 19 *Letterkenny* and No. 20 *Raphoe*. These locomotives (except No. 19) were also fitted with Livesey superheaters. In 1937 they were renumbered and named, No. 16 becoming No. 4 *Meenglas*; No. 17, No 5 *Drumboe*; No. 18, No. 6 *Columbkille*; No. 19, No. 7 *Finn*; and No. 20, No. 8 *Foyle*. The last class 5A was made up of three engines built in 1912; they too were 2-6-4 tanks and were fitted with Schmidt superheaters. They were No. 21 *Ballyshannon*, No. 2A *Stranorlar* and No. 3A *Strabane*. They were the first superheated narrow-gauge locomotives in

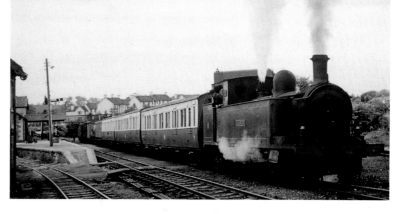

the British Isles and were renumbered and renamed in 1928 to become No. 1 *Alice*, No. 2 *Blanche* and No. 3 *Lydia*.

In recent years a great deal has been said and written concerning the CDRJC and its pioneering of the petrol and diesel railcar, and there is little doubt that this was one of the main reasons why the railway was able to hang on for as long as it did. In 1926 Henry Forbes, a man of great character, respected rather than liked by his staff, who had been the manager of the Joint Committee since 1910, introduced a passenger service using petrol railcars. This came at a time when the balance sheet was showing a need for lowering operating costs and Forbes decided that the time was ripe to show that his railway could operate a service equal to, if not better than, a road bus. This was done by using a 20-year old railcar that had been a permanent-way vehicle and by purchasing two railcars from the Derwent Valley line in England, the latter being converted from 4 ft. 8½in. to 3 ft. gauge. They were used to introduce a frequent service whereby passengers could be picked up and set down at halts, crossing-gates and other recognised stopping places. The scheme was an immediate success.

The Donegal was a pioneer in the introduction of diesel traction by rail. This was done with Nos 7 and 8 railcars, which went into traffic in 1931 between Strabane and Killybegs. From then on progress never stopped and better and more efficient railcars were continually being added, the last acquisitions being as late as 1951. The first passenger railcar was safely housed in the Belfast Transport Museum some time before the line closed.

Whilst it is true that Henry Forbes was only too conscious of the need for economies and that many of these, including the railcars, undoubtedly kept the line running, it is possible that this business of being parsimonious and catchpenny also ensured the end coming more quickly than might otherwise have been the case. One of the major reasons for closure at the end of 1959 was the state of the track – had this been renewed during the easier '20s and early '30s, bearing in mind that there were no shareholders, only two large owning companies, the tale might have been different. The railway was kept going by piece-meal closure of the Glenties and Londonderry branches after 1949 and salvaged material had to be obtained and used to keep the main line working. It was this and the surplus put by from the more prosperous working in the Second World War that kept the line running; when the surplus finally ran out they shut up shop.

One of the difficulties which beset both the Donegal and the Lough Swilly companies was the Border – a problem not affecting the smaller companies to the east and south. Even with efficient handling and examinations this meant delays, and thoughtless or rash passengers or negligent railway officials could make for delays of many minutes. What was worse, the towns and villages west of Strabane were virtually cut off from their old supply-point Londonderry, and began to develop a trade with the nearest large town in the Republic, Sligo, by road – this did not make for better financial results.

All lines were single throughout and were worked by electric train staff, using the miniature type instruments on the Finn Valley, West Donegal and Letterkenny lines, the others having the large type. The longest main-line section was 14 miles from Stranorlar to Lough Eske and the shortest from there to Donegal Town. At stations and halts other than electric train staff stations, sidings were operated by a key attached to the staff. The last vehicle on all trains carried a white tail-board by day and a red light by night. An unusual condition was that if a special train was to follow a scheduled one the former would

carry a red tail-board by day in lieu of a white one, or two red lights by night. If the special was running in the opposite direction a green tail-board was carried by day or one red and one green light by night. With the long single-line sections it was no easy matter to run the quite frequent railcar service integrated with goods trains and to run them to schedule, but it was done, and Donegal time-keeping was pretty good in spite of the additional operating worries of extra crowds in summer and bad weather conditions in winter.

Most of the interest in the Donegal has been in the post-war years, but after 1947 the rot began to set in and motor competition made itself felt. These were the years which ate into the contingency fund and when the policy of make do and mend became vital for survival. Even then it was a fight to the death and there was no apparent thought of surrender. The railcar stock was good, if a little like that of a Colonel Stephens railway in its variety, and these cars were used as much as possible, even for light goods-trains – it was essential to keep down the high cost of steam working as far as possible. One might deplore the supercession of steam, for steam is alive in a way that no other form of motive power can imitate, but the railway lived by the aid of this newer power and that was better than the alternative of no railway at all. Steam was still in existence on the heavier goods-trains and on summer specials, and it was to see these that the faithful came to Stranorlar in the summer months.

Even during the last year there was a regular steam goods service on the Strabane and Letterkenny section and also on the Finn Valley line to Stranorlar – occasionally this was extended to Donegal but the railcars could usually cope with the traffic beyond that point after 1957. Officially the trains were freight only but there was usually room for the favoured passenger in the large and smart red-and-cream bogie vans attached to the rear. There will be many who remember the two heavy freights from Strabane to Letterkenny and back, and the one return run from Strabane to Stranorlar. With luck the Finn Valley goods would continue over the bare and rugged terrain of the West Donegal, the exhaust slowing as they took the bank towards Meenglas and the climb to Barnesmore. On the days that they went on with an abbreviated train to Killybegs the duty was an exacting one, with a late evening arrival followed by an early start back the next morning in time to pick up the schedule of

2-6-4T *Blanche* leaves Donegal station.

2-6-4T *Blanche* pauses at Ballyshannon with the last excursion from Stranorlar on August bank holiday in 1959.

Meenglas leaving Donegal with an excursion train on 3rd August, 1959.

the next round trip at Stranorlar, perhaps with the same engine. This was tough going for the ageing McMenamin brothers, Jim and Frank, and they were the only Stranorlar crew left; during the winter months they never saw Killybegs by day for they arrived and left it during the long winter night. It was on one such morning that a Letterkenny crew, who had worked up with a special No. 6 and were returning home, got the green; they whistled and set off, and 'crash' they found themselves in the loco shed about 180 yards towards Donegal Town! But accidents were not in keeping with the Donegal, and even when the staff tried to make your hair stand on end with hints of the vacuum brake being a little unreliable, these stories somehow failed to ring true.

In a way, the Killybegs line could almost have been called the 'Donegal's' equivalent of the Burtonport Extension, though it actually followed the shores of Donegal Bay. Here the coast-line consists of a series of deep inlets between lofty headlands jutting far out into the sea, and the short level sections within sound of the sea were varied by a series of sharp rises and falls. These carried the railway over the spines of the headlands and made it a hard road to work, the engines laboring on the gradients as steep as 1 in 41, rocketing down equally steep descents and with squealing flanges lurching round the sharp curves in the manner of a fair-ground helter-skelter. The villages too had their own particular charms, Mountcharles (pronounced Mountcharless, just as Forbes was always called Forbess), Inver with its miniature signal cabin, its somersault signals and, down beyond the village where they still danced in the evenings at the crossroads, its hotel with a good table and German host; then there was Bruckless, with its small harbour, and finally the little covered station at Killybegs squashed between the town and the wall of its deep-water harbour. There was no engine turntable at Killybegs but beyond the water tower there was a railcar-table made, typically, out of the frames of one of the late-lamented 4-4-4 tanks.

In the later years the highlight of the steam workings were the holiday excursions to Ballyshannon, run at

Two old fashioned types of transport meet at Killygordon in Donegal. 4-6-4T Erne sporting geranium red colours meets more modern road transport in the goods yard.

weekends during the summer months; the last one of all ran on August Bank Holiday Monday 1959.

As in previous years trains ran from Strabane and Stranorlar using the entire available stock patched up and gathered together for the occasion. The heavier train was made up of *Blanche* and ten coaches running from Strabane, whilst the second train with seven coaches and *Meenglas* followed from Stranorlar; according to custom the dour and unsmiling locomotive inspector McBride accompanied the Strabane crew, the McMenamin brothers working the Stranolar special. Both trains were packed to the doors. In each case the first stop was Donegal with the need to reverse for the Ballyshannon Branch, and here the engines took water and made the most of the opportunity to clean their fires. Then, with the somersault signal pulled off they were away, taking the right-hand road leading to the undulating Ballyshannon Branch.

At Ballyshannon there was time enough for the excursion was not due to leave until the evening and having turned and watered the engines the crews had hours on their hands, though there was some consultation over *Blanche's* steaming, and it was decided that *Meenglas* would take the main train home to Strabane. On the return journey water was taken again at Donegal and *Meenglas* had her fire cleaned into the bargain before setting off in the low evening sunshine for the climb up through the Barnesmore Gap and on through Stranorlar to Strabane.

So in the event, the very last excursion of all was hauled by *Blanche*. The journey from Ballyshannon to Donegal was taken bunker first with a stop at Rossonwlagh to pick up a further crowd of passengers, and as the sun set they ran into the platform at Donegal. In a moment Frank McMenamin had eased up, his brother Jim had uncoupled and they were away over the crossing to run back through the platform road and back on to the water column for refreshment and fire cleaning; the opportunity was taken of opening the smokebox doors and shoveling out an accumulation of ash. This done, *Blanche* moved forward on to the main line, and backed on to the train; Jim checked the coupling and connected the vacuum 'bag', the signalman handed over the staff and they were away, *Blanche* vomiting black smoke as the red-and-cream train disappeared into the gathering gloom.

From Donegal the line rose steadily, though not yet spectacularly, towards the Blue Stack Mountains, the gradient becoming consistently steeper towards the staff section point at Lough Eske. Jim McMenamin got to grips with the bank straight away. Two shovelfuls at the front, and another in the middle, pause, two at the back, pause front again, pause, and so it went on, opening and closing the firebox door for each shovelful. He was using a fairly light fire and the needle kept steady, a plume of steam and smoke dropping away behind the train. In spite of McBride's fears, *Blanche* was steaming well and appeared to be in good nick, bar a rather nasty knock.

Once over the road crossing at Lough Eske the more scenic section of the climb began. Here the character of the line changed completely and having exchanged the miniature electric train staff with 'Paddy' the crossing-keeper, the train set off round the curve towards the lower reach of hills and away from the road; the climb here eased a little and the fire was checked and the boiler topped up just as they rounded the bend and crossed under the road by Barnesmore Halt. Here the 1 in 60 began and for the next three miles there was one of the most spectacular and dramatic sections of any Irish railway, the line clinging to slopes high above the road and river from which

the train appeared as a slow-moving model up against the mountain landscape. It was now dark, and looking down and back from the engine cab it was possible to see the headlights of the cars as they streamed up the black valley following the train; *Blanche* was throwing out great clouds of smoke and this drifted back and down towards them. Soon the road and rail came close together towards the summit; more cars were drawn up and hands waved as *Blanche* made her way along the high embankment, her train snaking behind her, the passengers waving also and entering into the spirit of the occasion. A few minutes more and they were under the Derg Bridge and making their way alongside the silver waters of Lough Mourne. The climb was over. Once again away from the road, the descent at 1 in 60 began, and for the next five miles the McMenamins took it easy, but kept their eyes on the darkness in front. All too soon the lights of Stranorlar came into view and air was allowed into the train pipe, round the curve and over the river they came, the train staff was handed to Pat Monteith at Stranorlar West Box and they drew to a halt at the east end of the platform. The crowds poured from the train and swarmed off into the darkness, Manager Curran checked that all was correct, *Blanche* took on water at the column and silence descended, the holiday was over.

They were great days, these Bank Holiday excursions, and even in the later times the crowds were heavy; generally it was a happy cheerful throng and the bottles were out and opened early. Barney Curran once told the story of the man who joined the Strabane excursion already the better for drink, and by the time they reached Stranorlar he was proving to be a bit of a nuisance. Curran had him out and put him on the engine with strict instructions to the loco crew that he was to be kept in front of the fire. It was a hot day, and by the time that they had fought their way up the bank and run down through the Gap with the fire-door open, he had had enough so they put him off at Donegal and never had any more trouble.

The last steam engine to work over the West Donegal section was the 54-year-old Baltic tank No. 14 *Erne*; again she was manned by the McMenamins, this time with Jim driving and Frank firing to him. Old Frank was put off driving towards the end as he did not pass the medical, but even so the two brothers continued to work as of old, Jim driving the engine through Stranorlar, just in case someone was watching, and once out of sight they went back to their former jobs. The date was 30th December, 1959, and they left Strabane with a long goods-train of supplies and coal for Ballyshannon; it was evening as they set off from Stranorlar, having waited for the last railcar to come over the long section from Lough Eske, and they headed for the Barnesmore Gap in the winter's darkness, the slow exhaust beat carrying across the quiet night into the homes of many who had spent their lives in the service of the railway.

There is one other story, and again it is of steam and the McMenamins. The final run out of Killybegs, on the last day of 1959 was made by railcar No. 12; she was scheduled to run right through to Strabane in accordance with normal practice. As the evening drew on and the mails had gone down to Strabane in rail-car No. 16 the crowds began to turn up in force at Stranorlar and it became clear that no railcar would be able to cope with the traffic, so Curran decided that the last passenger train of all would be hauled by steam. This was made up of five coaches and 2-6-4 tank No. 5 *Drumboe*, manned by the McMenamins; they left 20 minutes later and disappeared into the drizzling darkness to a chorus of exploding detonators. When they arrived back in Stranorlar both the brothers were actually in tears, overcome with emotion – for them it really was the end, and a lifetime's work on the engines was finished. The next day, New Year's Day 1960, Frank left the service; Jim was kept on as a lorry loader but as he said, it would never be the same again.

There was no question of failing to serve the public up to the last possible minute – the railway went down fighting, its last secretary and manager, the careful, meticulous and courteous Bernard Curran, carrying out the Forbes tradition to the very end. In his own hand he wrote the words which could well be taken as a fitting epitaph.

"When we cease operations on 1st January, 1960 one of the largest narrow-gauge systems in Great Britain will be gone, but with the growth of the motor-car and motor-lorry this was inevitable and we have carried on for as long as was possible. At least I can say that we have provided a service to the people of Donegal and will continue to do so as a road organisation. Our history has been well recorded by the railway historians and the photographs of our line must now be legion – so we shall not be forgotten."

Above: **The very last excursion of all was hauled by** *Blanche* **on the journey from Ballyshannon to Donegal. The McMenamim brothers on her footplate get to grips with the 1 in 60 grade up through the famous Barnesmore Gap.**

County Donegal railcar No.10 at Stranoarlar station.

VICTORIAN

These photographs are all taken in the current decade and present an impression of a railway built in the 1870s and still in Government ownership. The three foot gauge Isle of Man Railway is one of the railways in the British Isles remaining most faithful to the Victorian era. The pictures also represent another facet of our diverse hobby as they were all taken of special trains on photo charters with train formations created especially for the purpose.

Most of the pictures were taken in either April 2010 or 2011 on the Douglas to Port Erin Line of the Isle of Man Railway and show *G.H.Wood* in green

No.8 *Fenella* and No.13 *Kissack* prepare to leave Douglas in the late afternoon. Douglas station has been shorn of its platform canopies and second island platform.

livery and *Fenella*, *Loch* and *Kissack* in Indian red livery.

These engines were all built by Beyer Peacock in Manchester between 1874 and 1910 to a similar design, all with a 2-4-0T arrangement. The railway originally had 16 such similar engines (with No. 16 *Mannin* being a larger example of the type). The railway is unusual in remaining faithful to one locomotive builder and one basic type of steam engine throughout the long life of the railway. Eleven of the original engines remain on the Island, although not all in railway ownership.

Since its opening in 1873, the railway has played a leading role in the development of the Island as a tourist resort. It ran lines from Douglas to Port Erin and Peel. The Manx Northern Railway opened a line from St. John's (on the IoMR's Peel line) to Ramsey and also a branch to Foxdale but was taken over by the IoMR in 1905; *Caledonia*, a Dubs 0-6-0T and 'the Foxdale branch coach' remain on the IoMR as the only remaining working examples of that railway's equipment. *Caledonia* has returned to steam this year and is available for engine driving courses.

The 1950s created a boom in holiday traffic before the advent of cheap Mediterranean air flights and traffic peaked at one million passengers a year. However, by the 1960s. the railway was in decline as a result in significant loss of tourist traffic. Whilst the Welsh narrow gauge preserved lines were still booming, the British public did not often make the boat trip across the sea to Douglas and things looked grim for all the Island's railways which had remained

ISLAND

in a virtual time warp, including the Manx Electric Tramway and the electrified Snaefell Mountain Railway.

A fairy Godfather in the form of Lord Ailsa appeared on the scene and took a lease of the whole railway in 1967. All the lines were opened or re-opened and much paint was consumed in re-liverying all the engines in earlier green lined out in black & white. Traffic did not improve and Ailsa threw in the towel after only 18 months, but his appearing on the scene was for just long enough for the railways to get on the Island's political agenda. It became clear that complete closure could not be allowed as the railways were core to the Island's tourism and so economic infrastructure and employment.

After a few ups and downs, the Government has now taken a grip on the position and both supported and developed the three railway systems, although only the Douglas to Port Erin line has survived on the steam railway. Much has been refurbished and renewed, not least the track and permanent way. The steam engines have received considerable attention with several new boilers being fitted. No.4 *Loch* has run on the Manx Electric Railway and *Caledonia* has even run on a section of the Snaefell Mountain Railway. Maybe more extra-ordinary events will unfold in the future as No.1 *Sutherland* was returned to service for a short while using No.8 *Fenella's* boiler and whispers are appearing about the possibility of returning the larger and unique No.16 *Mannin* to service, although that would be a major repair job if not almost a complete renewal.

> **The many visitors to the Isle of Man are generally accustomed to the standard gauge railway of the mainland of Britain, so when for the first time they set eyes on the narrow gauge railway of the Island, with its small, but finely designed and built engines, they are fascinated by the system and its peculiar equipment.**
>
> *Ian Macnab in the opening lines of his Preface to his* History of the Isle of Man Railway, *published in January, 1945.*

Left: **David Williams** (who organises the charters) leaves no stone unturned to ensure photographers get the results they want. Here No.4 *Loch* and No.13 *Kissack* storm past the line up (for the seventh time!) just outside Douglas.

No.8 *Fenella* poses with a mixed train formation; technically inaccurate as goods wagons were historically on the back of the train, but, as they are only vacuum piped not braked, modern regulations require them to be at the front.

Middle left: **No. 8 Fenella** shunts at Castletown with two of the railway's only three remaining operable wagons.

Middle right: **No. 8 Fenella** and **No. 4 Loch** climb into Santon and its palm tree-lined platform.

Bottom: **Aisla green-liveried No. 10 G.H. Wood** runs past the wooden Port St. Mary signal with a train of saloons.

"Long may admirers of this unique little railway be able to enjoy the early morning whistles of the locomotives in and about Douglas, or the cheery echoes from Greeba Mountain as the locomotive signifies its approach to Cooillingill crossing, or the final triumphant shriek over the flats by Lezayre and Milntown as the train coasts into Ramsey terminus.

Ian Macnab in his *Conclusion.*

No. 8 *Fenella* takes water at the column, intriguingly placed inside Douglas shed, before her morning's work.

Top left: **No. 10 G.H. Wood** runs into Colby as the crew exchange line tokens with the station master.

Middle left: **No. 13 Kissack** takes water at **Balasalla.**

Lower left: **No. 13 Kissack** runs into **Port St. Mary.**

Below: **MNR No. 4 Caledonia,** in the deeper **Manx Northern Railway** red, returned to service in 2013, stands alongside **No. 8 Fenella** with the driver oiling up ready for departure from Douglas.

Narrow Gauge
Empire

In the far north of Burma, an area normally out of bounds to tourists without a special permit, a two foot system runs to service the Namtu silver mine. Here we see 99 year old Kerr Stuart 0-4-2T No.13 starting the climb round the spiral up through Wallah Gorge to the tippler plant on a charter in December 2011.

Fairlie had seen to it by the 1870 demonstrations of his patent double engine *Little Wonder* on the Festiniog Railway that narrow gauge railways had their place. Many people agreed with him, especially when they were seeking to save cost and open up foreign countries as quickly as possible, so as to extract minerals and gain a return. Narrow gauge lines sprang up all over the place and British industry loved it. They could hardly manufacture equipment fast enough.

One of the early lines 'off the block' and the first to open up Africa was the Beira Railway. Cecil Rhodes was keen to open up a route to the sea from Rhodesia, at the same time as driving three foot six inch 'Cape gauge' up from South Africa towards the Congo. He engaged well known African contractor, Pauling, to build a two foot line from Beira, now on the Mozambique eastern coast of Africa) to Umtali, the most eastern town in Rhodesia. This line was always going to be upgraded to the 'Cape gauge', but the thing was to build it as quickly as possible. The Beira area was swampy and mosquitoes carried off hundreds of railway workers until the line reached the highlands. Once construction was under way, it was realised that it was just too difficult to get the line to reach Umtali due to the mountainous terrain. So, Rhodes agreed that the town would come to the railway and compensated people to move; fortunately buildings were wooden and so

transportable by traction engines using logs as rollers put under the buildings to move them.

The motive power chosen for the line was a strange choice, although the steam engines were most attractive visually. Ideally, they would have been large eight or even ten coupled engines to haul long trains up the grade but, no, the Falcon works in Loughborough, England were commissioned to build a range of elegant 4-4-0 tender engines for the line. They coped somehow for the ten year life of the line and then were retired to sugar and other industrial lines when the railway was re-gauged, connected to the rest of Africa and became an integral part of the Rhodesia Railways empire. Several survive in Museums, notably one in the Bulawayo Railway Museum and two now restored to working order on the amazing Sandstone Estates narrow gauge railway in South Africa's Kwa Zulu Natal.

A flavour of the early life and times of this pioneer African but colonial railway can be gained from a contemporary account of a trip up the line: "We occupied one of the compartments, which was fairly comfortable, being provided with leather covered cushions, although they were burnt in places by sparks from the engine. The natives sat on top of the coal wagons and wrapped their blankets round them. There were about twelve white passengers on the train when we left. The little single track runs away across the veldt, the clearing through the grass, just being wide enough for the carriages to pass. It was a lovely morning, not too hot, whilst the novelty of the thing, and the feeling that at last we were right away from the every day world, was delightful... when about four miles out of Fontesvilla, there was more than the ordinary rocking and jolting, which is saying a great deal, and all at once we came to a standstill. Getting out, we found the front wagon had left the rails smashing three axle-boxes. All efforts to jack the derailed wagon onto the metals again failed. The locomotive steamed on to the next camp and brought back some 'boys'. They unloaded the whiskey, then pushing the empty wagon over out of the way, we coupled up and once more proceeded on our journey."

The railway line built up to Rhodesia from the Cape was a more serious affair and built to what has become known as the 'Cape gauge' of 3'6". The Beira Railway was quickly widened to this gauge and connected to the rest of the new international railway system running within South Africa, Rhodesia, Mozambique, Botswana, the Congo and Angola to form a complete network within Sub Sahara Africa. This system was provided with serious motive power. Straight away it ordered 4-8-0 tender engines from the North British Locomotive Works in Glasgow, but quickly went on to become one of the most profligate users of Beyer Garratt articulated locomotives, culminating in fast and free running 4-6-4+4-6-4 passenger and mixed traffic types and 4-8-2+2-8-4 heavy freight examples on Rhodesia Railways alone. It was quite usual to see 20 coach passenger and mail trains running daily. Even today, the much run down National Railways of Zimbabwe retains some half dozen working examples of Garratts used in Bulawayo shunting manoeuvres nearly every day.

Africa truly became a hunting ground for Garratt enthusiasts with many countries adopting the type. The famous East African Railway probably took the biscuit with the fabulously presented maroon liveried Class 59 Garratts designed very effectively to haul heavy freights up the escarpment from Mombasa to

Nairobi, often proudly worked by Indian Seiks who burnished and polished every part of the pride and joy they drove. Pretty much all the EAR locomotives were fitted with the Austrian Giesel ejector chimney design, supposedly to improve their efficiency; this it may have done, but at the cost of defacing their attractive appearance.

Africa was not the only part of the British Empire to benefit from railways of course. The great British Indian Empire was full of railways, stretching from the famous Kyber pass near Afghanistan to the diminutive two foot gauge railway which wound its way up the fragile Himalayan foothills to Darjeeling, reversing and twisting this way and that with circular loops and switchbacks to gain height from the hot and torrid plain at Siliguri (connecting with both the metre and broad gauge railways) to the tea estates of Darjeeling. Originally, this line was built so that the British civil servants and their army could escape the summer heat of Calcutta and recuperate in the cooler air. Of course, an Indian community has since built itself up in the region but not without subsequent political difficulty. West Bengal suffered from the 'thick red line' of colonial decision being drawn on the map to mark different administrative territories and, currently, the Gorkhaland community is striving to settle quasi-independence terms. Maybe this instability has been - and will yet prove to be - the saviour of the little 'toy train' which still runs with original design British steam engines, as it employs something in the region of 850 people. Now designated as a World Heritage site, it must be a thorn in the backside of Indian Railways but, so far at least, cash has been forthcoming to repair monsoon landslides and provide new equipment, although not always with the best results. Extraordinarily, a British-formed society named after the railway has taken upon itself to support the line and help its people and, recently, has shown the Tindharia workshop staff the way to repair the centenarian Scottish-built steam engines so they can continue to do their job of work on the 'Joy Train'

Umtali-bound freight train approaching a refuelling stop en-route with piles of neatly stacked logs waiting to be loaded as fuel.

Derailments were frequent on the Beira line due to the lightly laid track but easily rectified; such was the life of a pioneer colonial railway.

India's tourist promotion alongside the Himalayan range, the tiger and the Maharaja's palaces. But some quick and realistic thinking should take place to ensure the 'toy train' plays an effective role in its new and changing community and provides a 21st century service to indigenous and international tourists; surely, the original and capable steam engines should form a core part of any such plan.

India has several similar hill station towns, many with extant narrow gauge railways. Shimla, within relatively easy reach and a day's journey by train from Delhi, is a charming town clinging to the side of the lower mountains. It is reached by a long and winding 2'6" railway which retains all its original architectural features, including several triple arched viaducts, but is now run with modern and efficient diesel trains. However, for the princely sum of just 25 tickets, it is possible to hire a charming railcar, complete with whirring outside connecting rods, as a private train to take you on your own journey up through the hundred or so tunnels nearly to the clouds.

When Indians are being charitable about the British Empire and the days of the Raj, they will credit Britain with teaching them the English language and how to fight and also providing railways. India is covered with railways of all shapes and sizes in mainly three gauges: broad (5'6"), metre and narrow (mainly two foot), although the latter two gauges are dramatically reducing in scope. Apart from the hill station railways climbing to the sky, India had many wayside narrow gauge branch lines and some considerable networks. Calcutta had a huge network of two foot gauge commuter lines run by small tank engines. The Maharajah of Gwalior built a network of lines from his

from Darjeeling to Ghum, running up and around the famous Bhatasia loop (almost two complete circles to gain height) under the shadow of the mighty snow-capped Katchenjunga mountain. Almost everyone has heard of the Darjeeling Himalayan Railway and it is surely an incredibly worthwhile and key feature for

A ride up the Nariz del Diablo

Our engine, a 2-8-0, was built in 1955 by the USA firm of Baldwin-Lima-Hamilton with works number 75585 and railway number 53: sturdy but simple steam motive power, but one that meant business as we had a high mountain range to grapple with. No. 53's chime whistle echoed mournfully around the foothills as we barked away from Bucay across the Chanchan river and up through the forest towards the Andes. She was extremely clean. Her red-painted firebox protruded into the cab and her engine crew sat either side on a high platform. The regulator opened horizontally and, when the fogonero turned up the oil burner atomiser in the firebox, the flames licked around the edge of the firehole door. At Huigra, the station master handed over the paper train order to authorise our journey to Sibambe at the foot of the Devil's Nose mountain and we set off. The fireman threw two buckets of sand into the firebox, both instantly sucked through the tubes to lay a heavy pall of black smoke over the town as we forged ahead.

There were many tunnels on this section of the line and inside they were hot. No. 53 plunged into the

first black cavernous opening, the roar of her exhaust echoing back from the rock walls inside, the heat of the firebox flames were suffocating and scorching. Just as it was all too much, we burst out into the sunshine and the fresh mountain air and we gasped for breath. The mountain air seemed sweeter after that.

The Nariz del Diablo appeared at the end of the valley ahead of us, a curious conical shaped mountain up which the railway climbed by a series of switchback reversals; it had to, there was no other way out of the valley. Sibambe was at the foot of this climb and here we rested awaiting the down working of the daily 'mixto'. Before long there was a whistle from high

G&Q No. 44 hammers up the grade alongside the Chanchan river towards the Devil's Nose mountain switchbacks in Ecuador on 20th August, 1992.

home town with large eight-coupled tender engines, including a small 4-4-0 of his own to delight his guests. Indeed, he even created a model train made entirely of silver to run round the dining room table in his palace to deliver condiments and spices to guests' plates; they simply lifted the lid of the pot they wished to source from and this broke the electric current bringing the little train to a stand for the guest's convenience.

Not to be outdone, Sri Lanka once, and not so long ago, ran 2'6" gauge high pressure steam railcars made in Shrewsbury by a firm called Sentinel from the capital Columbo on the county's narrow gauge system; and such type is of particular interest to the ferro equinologist. Now, the narrow gauge lines have been ripped up, one Sentinel railcar remains capable of work, but only within the Columbo depot, rather like a caged lion in a zoo. English narrow gauge enthusiasts eye this last working survivor enviously and plot how they might repatriate it to the UK, but so far no-one has gone the whole hog to do so.

Empires and colonies built by other European countries also developed narrow gauge systems and often ordered British equipment, although engines from America and Germany encroached on the market. The Dutch islands of Indonesia ran many 3'6" gauge systems as well as smaller sugar cane lines. Many of the latter survive and, even now, some 60 steam engines can be seen hard at work bringing the sugar cane back from the fields each day in the season. Generally speaking, probably the majority of Indonesia's steam engines came from Europe; large 'mallets', huge 2-8-2s, ten-coupled rack tanks in Sumatra and diminutive tank engines and trams abounded to delight the enthusiast even as late as the 1980s. Perhaps two of the most

extraordinary British-made survivors were wood burning anachronisms from the later nineteenth century still working in their 90th years: the Sharp Stewart 2-4-0 B50 tender engines running in eastern Java from Madiun along the side of the road to the remote village of Ponorogo and the Beyer Peackock trams in Surabaya, built in the year of our Lord one thousand nine hundred and one. That a city's tram system still had one steam worked tramway running until nearly 1980 was truly remarkable, albeit only one train and with only one working tram engine! Whilst some of the steam trams had been put out to grass and the electric line closed, one steam tram soldiered on running a thrice daily train from the depot at Wonokrono on the outskirts of the city down to the harbour, fussily steaming alongside the main road and shrieking its high pitched whistle to warn street sellers to remove their wares from the trackside as it dived across the road down the branch line to the harbour. It even carried its valuable Beyer Peacock brass works plate right to the end.

East African Railways 59th class 4-8-2+2-8-4 Garratt No. 5901 in maroon livery on a freight at Nairobi.
(Photo: C. Gammell)

above and identical twin No. 38 see-sawed above us as she descended the inclines down to the station.

As soon as the single line was clear, No. 53 set off for its assault on the mountain, up the uncompensated 1 in 18 grade, with the engine barking fiercely and with her smoke shooting straight up towards the sky. Height was rapidly gained by means of these intriguing switchbacks: No. 53 ran into a dead end siding, immediately reversed, as the conductor simultaneously

threw the point switch behind the train, and pushed her train backwards up an even steeper section back past Sibambe station into a further dead end siding. Here the points were thrown once again and we forged ahead on up to Alausi, looking down at a toy-like Sibambe station far, far below and watching No. 38 roll her train down the mountain alongside the Chanchan river, the scene looking just like a model railway lost amongst the grandeur of the high Andes.

No. 53 had been fully extended for the dramatic climb; her regulator had been pushed wide open by the maquinista, the firebox hummed loudly under the pressure of the oil atomiser and her exhaust reached a crescendo. The whole locomotive shook and swayed like a banshee from hell, but she was now running free on the mountain ledge with the Devil's Nose behind her on up to the next challenge of the Alausi loops. This was narrow gauge railroading at its very best with men and machines masters of their task and one which they perform day in and day out.

Far left: 2-8-0 No. 44 climbs the switchback reversals on the Devil's Nose in Ecuador on 18th August, 1992.

Left: Identical twins Baldwin-Lima-Hamilton 2-8-0s Nos. 53 & 38 cross at Sibambe station at the foot of the Devil's Nose mountain on the Guayquil & Quito Railway in Ecuador in November, 1981.

Above: **Zimbabwe Railways Bulawayo shed at dawn in August, 1990 with four Garratts preparing for the day's work. From left to right: two 14th Class 2-6-2+2-6-2 Garratt Nos. 513 & 524, 15th Class No. 417 and 20th Class No. 735.**

Below: **A Darjeeling bound train climbs the grade circling round Chunbatti loop nearly twice to gain height before continuing up the mountain roadside. The engine is one of the famous B Class 0-4-0-STs hauling a train of early four wheeled carriages.**

Britain's most southerly continent, Australasia, was also full of steam engines and narrow gauge railways made in Britain. Perhaps the most famous is the Puffing Billy Railway, formerly a suburban branch from Melbourne but now restored as a preserved 2'6" gauge line and most popular running with American-made Baldwin locomotive works' 2-6-2Ts. Baldwin were a proliferate builder of narrow gauge locomotives to simple but rugged design. They were perhaps a builder who produced truly standard designs built to customer's order from a range of off the shelf parts which could largely be assembled as required. Indeed, Baldwins published a catalogue of locomotive types which could simply be ordered for delivery within weeks, which was the converse of much British locomotive building practice making bespoke designs. Any overseas railway operator could simply order an engine from the Baldwin catalogue and subsequently telex for spare parts using a pre-agreed code.

Both the North and South Americas had thousands of Baldwin and similar American Locomotive Company (ALCo) steam engines operating on their tough metre gauge lines in and around the Andes, but British locomotive builders too were successful in exporting particularly to South America where, frequently, entire railway systems would be designed and built under British influence, although mainly on the standard or broad gauge. Perhaps one of the most remarkable South American railway system (although it is hard to single out any one of the many) is the

Guyaquil & Quito Railway in Equador running from the sea up over switchbacks on the famous Devil's Nose mountain to Quito, high in the volcanic Andes mountains. Even as late as the 1950s, new rugged red-painted 2-8-0 steam engines built by Baldwin Lima Hamilton were being delivered and some still exist even today and are being refurbished to continue to run for tourists up the dramatic Chanchan river valley. To ride the roof of a train of box cars behind one of these oil fired locomotives must be one of the top ten steam narrow gauge railway experiences in the world.

Amazingly, when all had given up the G&Q for lost as an anachronism from the past, the President decreed that the line should be rebuilt, tourist trains introduced and even steam engines repaired. It is due to re-open in June this year so it still remains to be seen what actually happens, but this line is certainly one to watch as it is a life's 'must see and experience' even in rebuilt form. Don't miss it; use whatever is in your piggy bank to travel on it as it definitely shares with the Darjeeling Himalayan Railway the title of one of the world's top ten 'railways to experience before you die'.

The last of the empire steam experiences to describe is important because, equally unexpectedly, it brings the story right up to date and provides an experience which thankfully will continue for long into the future: the story of the NGG16 Garratts, their finale in South Africa and their extraordinary return to service, but in the northern hemisphere and in Wales on the Welsh Highland Railway.

Probably more that anywhere else, the African continent is synonymous with the Beyer Garratt locomotive type and, in South Africa these continued right up to the end and still run in preservation. The two foot gauge Garratts are famous for their operation on several of the Natal sugar cane lines running inland from the coast. The most extensive of these lines were the Port Shepstone to Harding (75 miles), Umzinto to Donnybrook (93 miles) and the Port Elizabeth to Avontuur (174 miles). The traffic carried required serious motive power and the NGG16 2-6-2+2-6-2 Garratts were developed to provide it, probably the largest two foot gauge engine built in the world. Beyer Peacock continued to meet the demand until its Gorton workshop closed, but the requirements for more engines continued and so the final batch was built by Hunslet Taylor in Johannesburg with the distinction of being the very last two foot gauge Garratt built in the world going to No. 156 in 1968.

Left: **Two DHR up trains negotiating the original reverse No. 1 (now reverse No. 3 as the track is often altered to avoid landslides on the mountain). The picture is thought to date from the 1920s, but was still available as a commercial postcard in Darjeeling in the 1940s.**

Gradually, the Natal lines were closed once road transport had been de-regulated, allowing significant competition for the first time. But enthusiasts saved the Port Shepstone to Harding line for a while and even built up the freight traffic with both logs and sugar cane until it too succumbed to road economics and,

perhaps, some politics. The fortune was the Welsh Highland Railway's, however, as the entrepreneurial minded rebuilders foresaw that the railway, as reconstituted and running through untamed wild Welsh mountain scenery, would command passenger numbers far higher than originally carried and, due to its much steeper gradients than the sister Ffestiniog Railway, different and larger locomotives would be required. Enter the NGG16s. Three were originally reserved and two arrived in Wales in working order, subsequently more being added to the fleet in following years. The 1 in 40 gradients of the WHR and

Far left: **A diagram of probably the most famous loop at Batasia. At 48 miles and nearly the summit of the line.**

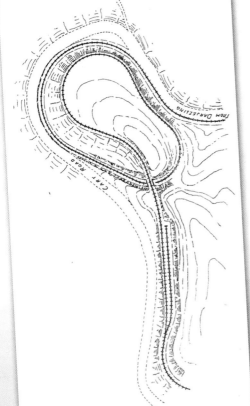

Mountaineer **on a rare freight train at Kurseong in September 1978.**

The 2'6" Kalka Shimla narrow gauge railway in steam days with a 'K' Class 2-6-2T on an up passenger train approaching Shimla. (Photo: P.S.A. Berridge)

An up train descends from the summit of the line at Ghum, running round the Batasia loop against a backdrop of the Himalayas on its last few miles run to Darjeeling.

NGG16 No. 153 reflections on the Sandstone Estates Railway in Kwa Zulu Natal in August, 2009.

trains of ten to twelve passenger carriages provided loads similar to the Alfred County which featured a steep climb up from the sea to an inland plateau, negotiating horseshoe curves and pulling 275 tons up the 1 in 45 grades at 25mph, co-incidentally the current maximum gradient of the WHR, although the original revival engineers had (and probably still have) 40mph speeds in their mind's eyes. So, the NGG16 Garratts live on in their second life, albeit in multi colours for tourists, labouring with long trains up steep hills, but masters of their work (unless wet Welsh leaves get the

better of them). They make fascinating comparisons with the Fairlie double engine and also the original England 0-4-0STTs of the Ffestiniog Railway. Also, due to foresight, the very last two foot Garratt built by Beyer Peacock, No. 143, can also be contrasted with the very first Garratt, K1, and on the same railway. Truly the F&WHR now provides a veritable feast of narrow gauge steam (and diesel) engine power on trains in daily service. And at gala events, these are often joined by some of the quarry 'racehorses' and even a vertical-boilered engine or two...

Right: **2'6" gauge Sentinel steam railcar** crosses the golf course on the outskirts of Columbo in Sri Lanka on 5th March, 1994. Sadly, the narrow gauge line is now closed and the railcar is confined to demonstration runs within Dematoga depot.

Top: Beyer Peacock wood burning steam tram B1221 crosses the road amongst the rickshaws in down town Surabaya in east Java in August, 1975. **Middle: NGG16 No. 153** at Valima on the Sandstone Estates Railway in Kwa Zulu Natal in August, 2009. **Bottom: Sharp Stewart 1880s built Class B50 wood burning 2-4-0** runs along the road side with the daily train from Madiun to Ponorogo in east Java in September, 1979.

NGG16 No. 143, the last Beyer Garratt built in England in 1958 now working daily on the Welsh Highland Railway in North Wales.

The developing role of

THE NARROW GAUGE RAILWAY

The essence of the industrial light railway, but in preservation days. De Winton vertical-boilered engine *Chaloner* blows off steam waiting in the loop at Stonehenge for a train hauled by a Kerr Stuart 0-4-0ST approaching from Mundays Hill on 30th October, 1971.

The Narrow Gauge Railway Museum Trust

Wharf Station TYWYN Gwynedd LL36 9EY

Registered Museum No RD 1433

Registered Charity No 1040128

RHEILFFORDD **TALYLLYN** RAILWAY

Not only was Birmingham the city where the concept of private British railway preservation germinated, but it was also one of the key locations where collections of narrow gauge locomotives started to gather. The Birmingham Museum of Science & Industry in Newhall Street was a particular magnet on wet winter afternoons as it had assembled a magnificent collection of industrial stationary and moving steam engines of all types, and steamed them frequently. As a small boy, it was wonderful walking around the exhibition halls watching fly wheels and beam engines revolve and heave themselves up and down and smell the oily steam. Of course, the Midlands could be said to be the birthplace of industrial Britain; subsequent developments at the open air museums at both Ironbridge and in the Black Country have taken this much further than could have been imagined in the 1950s.

After the second world war, narrow gauge railways disappeared very fast as new technologies and road transport quickly replaced them. Enthusiasts formed many societies to visit and photograph as many of these as possible. As the same thing was occurring on standard gauge and foreign railways as well, prioritising what to see and do was a tough task. Indeed, the National Collection concentrated on standard gauge equipment, save for a few narrow gauge industrial examples which had operated in the workshops at Crewe and Horwich on the 18inch gauge.

It was clear that some items should be saved for posterity and, often, owners and managers of industrial factories were sympathetic to the preservation cause, either giving away or selling engines - and sometimes even complete railway systems - for nominal sums. The first pressing question was where to keep these artefacts if the railway they came from had been torn up? Two solutions presented themselves early on in the 1950s: The Birmingham Science Museum itself and the Talyllyn Railway which started to draw to Towyn several really key items such as the Penrhyn vertical-boilered engine *George Henry*, the Welsh Highland Railway *Russell*

The Narrow Gauge Railway Museum Trust's information leaflet depicting *Dot* the 18 inch gauge works shunter at Beyer Peacock's Gorton Works.

Above left: **The National Railway Museum's contribution to narrow gauge railway preservation: *Wren* from the Lancashire & Yorkshire Railway's works system at Horwich, also built to 18 inch gauge and of a similar design to *Dot*, shown here at York and restored to L&YR lined livery.**

Above right: **Personal preservation: The Rev. Teddy Boston with his pride and joy, Bagnall 0-4-0ST *Pixie* which he ran on a short horseshoe railway round the Cadeby Rectory which was open to all.**

Lorna Doone, **Kerr Stuart 0-4-0ST built in 1922 for use by Devonshire County Council and shown here under restoration by the Birmingham Museum of Science & Industry.**

(which, fortuitously, had survived in working order at the Hook Norton and then at the Fayles industrial railway complex at Corfe Castle) and an engine from the Guiness brewery in Dublin. The Birmingham Museum gave a home to *Secundus*, the second steam engine from the Furzebrook Tramway in Dorset as it had originally been made in Birmingham. The City was far better known for its manufacture of carriages (particularly for export), but Bellis & Seeking built the one engine, an 0-6-0T to the unusual gauge of two feet, eight and a half inches. When the tramway was abandoned in 1955, the engine was bought for scrap by Ableson & Co of Birmingham and presented to the Birmingham Locomotive Society and then to the Museum. Intriguingly, Douglas Ableson was also the sponsor in purchasing an Andrew Barclay well tank from the RAF and presenting it to the Talyllyn Railway on condition it was named *Douglas* after him. It is clear that quite a lot of 'Birmingham persuasion' went on during the 1950s for the Birmingham Loco Club also rescued *Russell*. The City Museum also gave a home to two other narrow gauge steam engines, simply because it was an established Science Museum with a leaning towards steam engines through its curator Norman Bertenshaw. It acquired *Lorna Doone*, a 1922 Kerr Stuart 0-4-0ST from the Public Works Department of Devonshire County Council and also *Leonard* a Bagnall 0-4-0ST from the Birmingham, Thame & Rea District Drainage Board. And so the concept started.

Of course, once the Talyllyn Railway started to amass a collection of narrow gauge equipment, more and more items rolled in. Whether Towyn was the best place to have located such a museum may be doubtful, but the TR people are to be applauded for their efforts in saving so much and now a really super small museum has been established within the new building at Tywyn Wharf station which tells the narrow gauge story very well. Of

course, it isn't possible to do justice to everything, but the museum has a diverse number of interesting items, ranging from the Beyer Peacock 18 inch works shunter *Dot* (which, with its copper-capped chimney just has to be one of the most beautiful locomotives ever made), including *Jubilee 1897* from the *Penrhyn*, *Rough Pup* from Dinorwic and a Padarn four foot gauge transporter wagon complete with three two foot wooden slate wagons and a guard's van. Its collection is not limited to Wales and there are also a variety of Irish and English items (mainly artefacts: signals, nameplates, etc.), a Scottish gas works 0-4-0WT and, out on loan, a Sentinel steam engine *Nutty*, which ran on the Welshpool & Llanfair Railway for a time.

Following the success of re-establishing several of the Welsh narrow gauge railways as complete and restored entities and using them for a revived tourist purpose, this provided encouragement to save other lines, locomotives and equipment and, of course, much has been kept in private collections often picked up at the same time as items were gathered for the public collections. In recent times, some have raised a question mark about the ethics of this; who should have the right to decide what items are kept by private individuals and should they not all be in museums? We now see an increasing number of classic and important narrow gauge items coming up for sale at auction; for example a Leek & Manifold Railway nameplate and a Corris Railway number plate. However, we should comfort ourselves that so much has been saved and remember that when all these items were being thrown out as scrap that was exactly the position. All the items would have been melted down if not saved by the enthusiasm and time freely given by several individuals and it is hardly surprising that some kept choice items for themselves as they were also freely offered to them, often by people within the industry who were friends. We should be grateful for what has survived.

Preservation increased and became more diverse. Enthusiasts saved much of the Leighton Buzzard's sand railways and, after a side step to create a US Iron Horse Railroad, have now reverted to preserve much of the original line, although sadly considerable housing development has encroached in recent years. Nevertheless, it remains a delightful example of an industrial narrow gauge railway, weaving amongst the layout of a town, diving across roadways and running along hedgerows using equipment highly appropriate to its origins. A plethora of new lines and preservation centres have also been built up to preserve and operate all manner of industrial narrow gauge equipment; some have broadened out into industrial archaeological centres

such as the Amberley Chalk pits museum, formerly the collection started by the Narrow Gauge Railway Society which has recorded so much of the historical scene by preserving several engines there, and at the Leeds Museum, as well as establishing a very comprehensive research library.

Some new centres have grown up to develop and operate extensive private collections, notably the Statfold Barn Railway in the Midlands and the Bredgar & Wormshill Railway in Kent, and both these lines and other centres have repatriated and imported many locomotives as part of their growing collections - some coming from as far away as Indonesia, including the very last steam engine ever built by Hunslet, which was delivered to a sugar cane line in Java.

Generally speaking, the steam railway movement in Britain has grown and matured substantially. There is nothing it cannot achieve, including rebuilding long lost lines such as the Welsh Highland and the Lynton & Barnstaple railways. Whilst these recreations originally stem from the desire to rebuild something worthwhile and gain satisfaction from doing so, these new enterprises have often been able to attract much public sponsorship on account of the significant economic regeneration they achieve in otherwise depressed regions.

Through a doctoral dissertation at the university of Bangor, Dr Megan Williams undertook an analysis of the economic impact of he Ffestiniog & Welsh Highland railways on Gwynedd. This showed that the various funding authorities are getting an excellent return on their grant contributions. Her work showed that the railways have made a considerable contribution to the regional economy since their re-opening. Analysis of data shows that railway visitors and volunteers inject around £5,210,000 into the regional economy each year and that this leads to additional expenditure of between £781,400 and £1,562,900 by the people whose jobs they support. The data also shows that the railways inject some £9 million into the local economy overall and it is expected that this figure will grow as the WHR develops over time.

The WHR received some £10 million grant funding to enable it to be rebuilt as far as Rhyd Ddu and, thanks to the tourist traffic generated it has been returning some 80% of that sum to the regional economy annually. The report continues with an outstanding remark: "Construction started on the WHR in 1997. Since then, the total amount the Railways have collectively returned to the local economy... is estimated to be over £60 million. The overall contribution of the WHR to the regional economy from the cost of its construction alone, is in excess of £32 million".

These are amazing and important statistics and have a more significant impact on the sustainability of narrow gauge railways for the future than can at first be imagined. Hitherto, most of the restoration, refurbishment and development of narrow gauge (and other heritage) railways has been achieved by sheer hard work and pocket money from dedicated individuals to ensure that something of the past is retained for enjoyment today and for tomorrow. Now, provided it can be shown that such railways and endeavours contribute significantly to the regeneration of the region they are in, further capital development sums may be available to improve and develop them and help ensure that, once again, the narrow gauge railway has a part to play in the life and fortunes of a country. Ironically, the purpose of such railways is now in the tourist market rather than concerning the extraction of minerals for which they were created.

However, despite these successes, all such heritage railways (irrespective of size, gauge or standing) require a continuous supply of human endeavour on a voluntary basis to ensure their sustainability. Very few can remain profitable purely using paid staff. The Ffestiniog Railway has recognised this and, over the years, has put in a great amount of effort to encourage the next generations of volunteers to experience and learn about its railway, its history and its modern day operations and has reached out to ensure this remains the case. Every summer it sponsors and manages a Kids' Training Week on the railway to help instil deep interest in the railway within young volunteers. So successful is this enterprise that the railway is now attracting its fourth generation of family volunteers. Data available for 2008 showed that around 80,000 volunteer hours were worked on the railway. At a conservative value of £10 per hour, this means that the value to the railway of volunteer work that year amounted to some £800,000. Something that is essential to the continued well-being of the railway.

These are most important issues; much more important than celebrating the 150th anniversary of narrow gauge steam engines or reviewing some of the eccentric past history of our narrow gauge lines. If it can be the case that some of our modern day steam heritage and tourist railways can attract such a sustainable number of volunteers annually and, also, make significant economic contributions to the area in which they operate, then all the endeavours to resurrect some of our historic narrow gauge lines will be worthwhile and many of our future generations will be able to experience, benefit and enjoy them. That is surely more than their promoters ever imagined.

The Ffestiniog Railway and its people who make it tick. Engines rebuilt, conserved and new (but all with heritage appearances) line up at Porthmadog Harbour Station during the annual end of season heritage weekend with dedicated volunteers who, with all their colleagues, contribute over 80,000 hours of free time annually to ensure the railway remains sustainable.

Postscript

"People from many walks of life have discovered a new and immensely satisfying way of spending a holiday in surroundings of great beauty. But they have also done much more than this. Not only have they the satisfaction of knowing that their efforts have given an historic line a new lease of life, but they have given pleasure to the many holiday-makers who travel over it each summer" L.T.C. Rolt

The Snailbeach Railway engine shed in Shropshire, long since abandoned, but still complete and with track remaining in situ had been a place of pilgrimage for enthusiasts for years. The whole mine site has recently been tastefully conserved, repaired and interpreted without wholesale renewal or change, so retaining its innate charm as an abandoned railway and mine system.

ENDPIECE & *Acknowledgments*

This publication is a celebration rather than a history or a definitive work, although the opportunity has been taken to update some previous historical reporting with more recent research material, perhaps casting a somewhat different aspect to previous assumptions and beliefs. In relation to some of the preservation activities since the second world war, occasion has also been taken to make some comments which some may consider challenging or even 'on the edge' about some recent historical and current activities and prospects, but why not? Apart from hoping you will enjoy the essays and pictures, if your mind is also set thinking about the status quo and future prospects of narrow gauge steam railway in the British Isles, so much the better. History will not stop today and those responsible for the future of narrow gauge railway preservation will have the opportunity - if not the obligation - to redress some of the ills bestowed upon existing lines out of expediency at the time, but which need not always remain so.

One of the problems with writing history is that authors were, by definition, not around at the time and so cannot possibly know all the whys and wherefores, even if a detailed trawl is made through the record books. To take just one example, consider the GWR's decision to buy the Corris which, in just one meeting, moved from no to yes; what was the mind changer? Probably the Bristol Tramways Company's canniness in offloading a loss-making part of its business at the same time as its crown jewels..

Even contemporary writing can have its issues, as Gordon Rushton found out when writing his Welsh Highland Renaissance book which covers the rebuilding of the WHR more as a current affairs record. The issue with that is people even see the present differently. The WHR construction board had three Michaels and a Malcolm on it and, unless one got all four people in a room to agree a story, each one would tell a different version. Such is life; people are different, but this causes the historian and even the recorder of current affairs considerable difficulty which has to stand criticism as soon as the ink is dry.

So, this publication is neither a history or a current affairs record. It is a celebration and tells some stories (as accurately as I can) to give a flavour of the narrow gauge, its contribution to Britain, its industry and, more recently, holiday experiences and the significant preservation and development movement which has grown up over the last 60 years.

The observant reader will have noticed that railway and place name spellings vary throughout the text. This is deliberate. Names change over time for many reasons.

I have used the spelling relevant for the time, even if that changes within an individual essay; everything evolves.

Some text has been taken from two classic PBW narrow gauge books but augmented, edited and refreshed. Narrow Gauge Album and On the Narrow Gauge are both classics of their time, but only now obtainable in second hand bookshops. Some of the text deserves a wider and more popular readership, alongside interesting photographs and with some annotations.

One common theme as true today as it was in PBW's time was his acknowledgment to my mother who often accompanied him on frequent visits to these little railways and also took pictures as well when PBW wanted more than one image of a moving train at a particular location. The same is true of the current and third generation as my wife Helen and twin boys Russell and Stuart have also enjoyed trips on many of the narrow gauge railways which survive, often combining a ride with a day's walk and picnic accompanied by one of our dogs as a typical British day out. Helen and Russell also have helped assemble this bookazine and Stuart is as interested in the narrow gauge as anyone. All this has given me a deep and satisfying pleasure too in having my interest shared by my family, just as it did PBW. And now we are into the third consecutive generation.

The very final word accompanies the postcard of the Southwold Railway on this page which features a train at Southwold station with one of the Sharp Stewart 2-4-0Ts and the carriages probably originally intended for the Chinese Woosung Railway. My mother's family come from Suffolk and their name was Heyward. One of the family was stationmaster at Southwold. It is lovely to have a real family narrow gauge connection...

Michael Whitehouse

> "Those responsible for the future of narrow gauge railway preservation will have the opportunity - if not the obligation - to redress some of the ills bestowed upon existing lines out of expediency at the time, but which need not always remain so"

Postcard of Southwold station.

Acknowledgments: John Adams, Hugh Ballantyne, P.S.A. Berridge, Caernarfon Records Office, W.A. Camwell, F.C. Carrier, Ken Cooper, A.W. Croughton, John Dobson, Maurice Earley, Alfred Fisher, C.Gammell, J.A. Ingram, Jim Jarvis, G.D King, H.J.King, Industrial Railway Society, Sidney Leleux, Ian Macnab, B.R. Molineaux, T. O'Brien, Ivo Peters, Richard Rolt, Pat Whitehouse, W.H. Whitworth, Glenn Williams; all other pictures (including some of the above) are from the Editor's collection. Thanks also to Carole Underhill for her patient typing.